winning women's bodybuilding

winning women's bodybuilding

Laura Combes
with Bill Reynolds

Contemporary Books, Inc.
Chicago

Library of Congress Cataloging in Publication Data

Combes, Laura.
  Winning women's bodybuilding.

  Includes index.
  1. Bodybuilding for women. I. Reynolds, Bill.
II. Title.
GV546.6.W64C65   1983   646.7′5   82-22039
ISBN 0-8092-5616-9 (pbk.)

All exercise and uncredited photos by John Balik, printed by Isgo Lepejian.

Copyright © 1983 by Laura Combes and Bill Reynolds
All rights reserved
Published by Contemporary Books, Inc.
180 North Michigan Avenue, Chicago, Illinois 60601
Manufactured in the United States of America
Library of Congress Catalog Card Number: 82-22039
International Standard Book Number: 0-8092-5616-9

Published simultaneously in Canada by
Beaverbooks, Ltd.
150 Lesmill Road
Don Mills, Ontario M3B 2T5
Canada

contents

	introduction	vii
chapter one	**woman bodybuilder**	1
chapter two	**fundamentals of women's bodybuilding**	7
chapter three	**intermediate techniques**	21
chapter four	**chest exercises**	35
chapter five	**back exercises**	43
chapter six	**shoulder exercises**	51
chapter seven	**leg and abdominal exercises**	61
chapter eight	**arm exercises**	79
chapter nine	**bodybuilding routines**	93
chapter ten	**competitive techniques**	113
chapter eleven	**the complete cycle**	153
	index	167

Laura Combes, Ms. America. *(Bill Reynolds)*

introduction

This book is an advanced bodybuilding training manual intended for use by women interested in bodybuilding competition. As such, it skips over numerous beginning- and intermediate-level bodybuilding concepts and techniques. Just as one example, I expect readers to understand the basic terminology of weight training and bodybuilding before attempting to read *Winning Women's Bodybuilding*.

Women who are unfamiliar with weight training and bodybuilding should read one or more basic books on the subject before tackling the information and techniques presented in *Winning Women's Bodybuilding*. One book I have consistently recommended in the past is Frank and Christine Zane's *The Zane Way to a Beautiful Body* (Simon & Schuster, 1979). Many of the

Laura Combes and Bill Reynolds.

introduction

exercises I use in my own training programs were learned from reading the Zanes' book. My co-author, Bill Reynolds, has previously written two basic unisexual weight training books that could help you, the *Complete Weight Training Book* (Anderson-World, 1976) and *Weight Training for Beginners* (Contemporary, 1982). You might also find Betty and Joe Weider's *The Weider Book of Bodybuilding for Women* (Contemporary, 1981) to be valuable.

Your relative physical condition will also have considerable bearing on how you use this book. Before you attempt to use even the least intense training routine outlined in Chapter 9, you will need to have at least three or four months of intensive preconditioning with weight training behind you. Any less than that, and your muscles will become incredibly sore and you'll soon overtrain. I don't think any woman bodybuilder could make gains on my personal routine as outlined in Chapter 11 without a minimum of two or three years of consistently hard training under her belt.

As you read this book, please keep in mind that I am writing about what works well for me, and for other supermuscular women bodybuilders. That doesn't mean that everything I write will work equally as well for you. Every woman's body reacts uniquely as a result of exposure to external training and dietary stimuli. One of the beauties of bodybuilding is that you alone must search through all of the exercises, routines, and training techniques available to you in order to discover what works best for your unique body.

Good luck with your search!

Laura Combes
Ms. America
July, 1982

winning women's bodybuilding

**To my mother
  for loving
To my family
  for believing
To my friends
  for enduring**

chapter one
woman bodybuilder

I am a woman bodybuilder! And as a woman bodybuilder I feel happier and more fulfilled than I have at any other time in my life. I will no doubt be training until the day I die.

Personally, I am the type of woman who enjoys responding to a challenge, and bodybuilding is far and away the most challenging sport I've ever practiced. I've been on Collegiate National Champion teams in water skiing and rugby, and bodybuilding is a much more demanding sport than either. Not only do bodybuilders train as hard (or harder!) as athletes in any other sport, but we frequently do so on a severely calorie-restricted diet, completely the opposite of what most other athletes do.

We also are at the mercy of a subjective judging system. Even though I may be in my lifetime best bodybuilding condition, the style of my physique may not appeal to a judging panel. Depending on the composition of the judging panels, I could enter two shows in exactly the same shape, placing first in one and tenth in the other. Obviously, such a situation can break or build a lot of character.

The bodybuilding lifestyle challenges your own personal strengths—something that greatly appeals to me. I am constantly self-tested to see how close I can push myself to my absolute physical and mental limits. And, in virtually every workout I *am* extending my physical limits. If I wasn't, I wouldn't continue to improve as a bodybuilder.

I also enjoy the fact that bodybuilding is an individual sport, so I win or lose on my own merits, rather than on the performance of teammates. Every time I see improvement in my physique, I am a winner. As a result, I compete only against myself to improve for most of the year, then compete against other well-muscled women bodybuilders only once or twice a year.

THE ESTHETICS OF BODYBUILDING

Bodybuilding is not only a sport, but an art form. I think of my posing onstage at a competition or exhibition as a display of kinetic sculpture. Of course it's not as easy to add muscle mass to my shoulders as it is for an artist to slap clay on the shoulders of a statue, but the end result is the same. And, I can move while onstage. A statue is rigidly fixed in one posture.

In bodybuilding most athletes are self-coached, so there is considerable opportunity to develop a high degree of self-discipline that transfers well into other areas of one's life. We also are involved in a sport of patience, which adds to one's self-discipline. Muscles grow in size quite slowly, so patience is indeed a virtue that every competitive bodybuilder must possess.

You should always have one primary goal as a self-coached athlete: to exceed your previous best condition in each succeeding contest. And when you manage to do this, you are genuinely a winner, whether or not you actually take home a trophy. In terms of improving health and strength, building self-discipline, and

Rachel McLish (1980 and 1982 Miss Olympia) placed second and Laura, fourth, in the 1981 Olympia. *(Mike Neveux)*

developing a healthy attitude toward hard work, everyone is a winner in bodybuilding.

As your physique improves, your self-image will also improve. I've seen scores of timid, dependent, and introverted women develop into self-reliant, aggressive, and highly motivated individuals as a result of regular bodybuilding training. Be cautious as your self-image improves, however, that you don't lose your ability to criticize yourself. A bodybuilder who is unable to see the weaknesses in her physique will never become a champion.

Over the long haul, the main benefit that you will derive from regular bodybuilding training is a lifetime of buoyantly good health. The bodybuilding lifestyle emphasizes regular vigorous exercise, the maintenance of a health-promoting diet, and the development of a positive mental attitude. These three factors are at the very heart of what leads to a long, clean, healthy, and happy life.

THE KEEN EDGE OF COMPETITION

I love bodybuilding competition, and I am motivated to train super-hard for an entire year by the thought of competing in the Miss Olympia show. And I don't compete in a beauty contest or freak show, since every woman onstage at the Olympia is an experienced and dedicated *athlete*.

Because I love to compete, I enjoy my training more. I love being onstage posing and hearing the audience's applause. The audience applauds because they know a good physique when they see one, and they know how much training, sacrifice, and self-discipline has gone into developing that physique. The judges may see one thing in your physique and the audience quite another, so sometimes the audience is a better barometer of how you appear onstage than the judges. Their applause thrills me to the core of my existence as a woman bodybuilder.

Onstage, the burden is entirely on you to display your physique to its best advantage. The judges aren't able to know how hard you trained and dieted for a particular competition. They only see how you appear onstage. So if you don't have great compulsory poses and an effective free-posing routine, you have only yourself to blame.

I've seen inferior physiques beat superior physiques through outstanding posing presentation, charismatic stage presence, tenacious competitiveness, and an iron will to win. Competition can bring out the best or worst in you, and you must be in total control of which facet of your bodybuilding persona is made evident to the judges and audience.

While you can learn quite a bit about yourself at a competition by comparing yourself with others in the show, your primary concern should always be in comparing yourself to your previous self. No one can stop you from training like a maniac to improve, but many people in the sport enjoy making snide remarks about truly muscular women bodybuilders. Don't worry about what others say or think. Please *yourself* by training super-hard and building a great physique.

At the highest level of women's bodybuilding, the sport can provide a professional athlete with a lucrative income. And as the

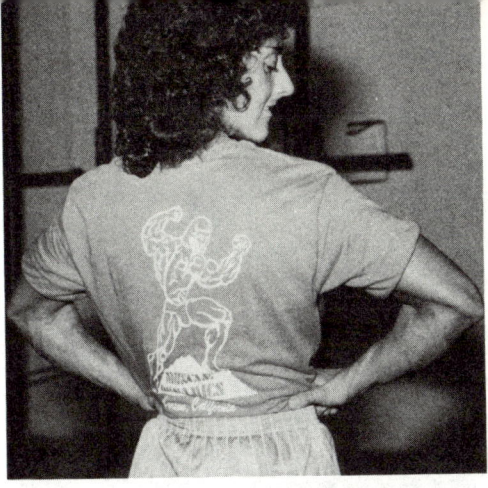

woman bodybuilder

Laura displays a T-shirt with the logo of her sponsor, Muscle Dynamics.

sport continues to grow in popularity with the public, it will become more lucrative to women further down in the bodybuilding hierarchy of champions.

As a successful professional bodybuilder, I derive my income from competition prize money, product endorsements, training seminars, posing exhibitions, personal appearances, coaching upcoming bodybuilders, sales of photos and T-shirts, writing magazine articles, and writing books like this. I certainly don't make the money a pro tennis player or golfer banks, but I do have a good income from bodybuilding. And, as bodybuilding continues to explode in popularity, every professional bodybuilder will be able to make more from the sport.

BODYBUILDING FOR EVERYONE

Bodybuilding is for every woman, regardless of age or initial physical condition. I even know several physically handicapped women who enjoy bodybuilding training several times a week. Any woman with at least partial use of her arms or legs can pump iron with light weights and profit greatly from the added physical activity.

Even if you never step onstage to compete, you will reap wide-ranging physical and mental benefits from following a bodybuilding lifestyle. Your improved appearance will radiate from your body, and everyone will notice it. Instead of being word-of-mouth, bodybuilding is a word-of-*eye* activity. Seeing is believing, and everyone can appreciate someone who is in superior physical condition. So, get into a gym and pump some iron!

1981 Miss Olympia contest. *(Mike Neveux)*

chapter two
fundamentals of women's bodybuilding

While there is no doubt that women's bodybuilding has experienced explosive growth in popularity since its inception in 1978–1979, the sport has been burdened by an inability of officials to establish consistent judging criteria. Literally no one seems to have a clear idea of what a woman bodybuilder should look like. For every woman like myself who feels she should have good proportions plus massive and well-defined muscles, there is another who feels that women bodybuilders should be smooth-looking and have a minimum of muscular development. My own exodus through the sport can serve well to illustrate how judging standards have vacillated over the years.

When I first heard of women's bodybuilding in late 1978, the idea of getting into a bathing suit and showing my body to a panel of judges and crowds of spectators made me laugh out loud. As an athlete, I just couldn't understand it. A majority of women today still can't understand the appeal of bodybuilding.

At that point I already had a great deal of muscular development as a result of my participation in athletics and several years of moderately intense weight training to improve my athletic performance. Ten years of water skiing had developed my back, shoulders, biceps, and thighs. Playing rugby had further improved my physique, particularly my calves, and weight training had brought all of my muscle groups even further along. By any standards, I was a very well-developed woman athlete.

One of my friends, Lynn Scull, had seen a poster in the University of South Florida weight room advertising a Ms. Brandon bodybuilding contest to be held in March 1979. (Brandon is a city on the outskirts of Tampa.) Because of my obvious muscular development, Lynn suggested that I enter the competition. Since I considered the concept to be so radical, I just shrugged off her suggestion, saying, "Nah, no way."

Tragically, in February 1979, Lynn was killed by a drunk driver. She had been such a good rugby player that I felt her

Laura played scrum half for a collegiate national rugby team (University of South Florida). Here she is shown in action throwing a "dive pass." Nice action shot, eh? *(Dick Falcon)*

8

fundamentals of women's bodybuilding

death was a terrible waste of athletic talent. I wanted to do something athletic to honor her memory, and for a couple of years I had been casting about for an individual sport in which I could compete, so I decided to enter the Ms. Brandon competition after all.

I had one problem, however—I didn't know the first thing about bodybuilding posing. My boyfriend at the time suggested I go to Hector's Health Studio in Tampa to talk to the owner, Hector Morales. Hector agreed to help me and showed me films of Ed Corney posing. Corney was the best male poser of the day, and I modeled my routine after his, not knowing that women's bodybuilding officials would consider my routine to be "too masculine."

From the very first, I was out to prove a point that women bodybuilders should have *muscles*—and *big ones* at that. I also felt that any bodybuilder, man or woman, should be able to effectively display his or her hard-earned muscular development. With this attitude versus the beauty-contest attitude of the officials, I caused quite a ruckus by entering that competition. They even forced me to compete in high heels. In what other sport do you compete in heels? I'd have felt more comfortable competing on stilts!

As the only real bodybuilder in the show, I placed fourth. Everyone above and below me was a pencil neck. But the audience had gone totally berserk when I did my double-biceps, side-chest and most-muscular poses, so I felt I'd made my point. Unfortunately, the Ms. Brandon 1979 officials couldn't handle the way I looked or the way I posed.

By the time I competed in the Best-in-the-World Championships in the late summer of 1979, officials had agreed to forbid me to pose "like a man," (e.g., with closed hands). I stuck to my guns, however, and I went ahead and continued with my posing style and heavy training. To me, bodybuilding still meant *muscles* and I was hell-bent to get them. As a result, I went through a string of contests in which I'd win "Most Muscular," "Best Muscle Tone," and/or "Best Poser," but wouldn't place in the top four or five.

Ms. Brandon contest (April 29, 1979): Laura's first bodybuilding competition. The winner was Kathy Lewis (second from right). Georgia Fudge (left) and Pam Brooks (between Fudge and Combes) are still competitively active. Sorry, but Laura has no idea who the woman on the right is. *(Dick Falcon)*

A breakthrough came for me in late 1979 and early 1980, when I won the Ms. Tampa and Ms. Northwest Florida titles. I met Richard Baldwin, twice Mr. America in his class and twice a second-place finisher in the Mr. Universe competition. Richard was one of the first major male bodybuilders to come out in favor of a muscular look for women. He took me under his wing and within a year had taught me everything about bodybuilding training and diet that had taken him a lifetime to learn.

I improved dramatically as Richard's training partner, and in May of 1980 won the Ms. Florida title. A year before I'd placed fifth in the Florida. I'll never forget the looks on the faces of Mike and Ray Mentzer, the show's guest posers, as I went through my free-posing routine. They were looks of utter astonishment. Mike later came backstage and told me I'd astounded him. Mike's words of encouragement got me really psyched up to win the America in September.

At Santa Monica, California, the world's bodybuilding capital, I entered and won the Ms. America competition. Richard Baldwin also won his class, so we were quite jubilant. We made bodybuilding magazine covers worldwide and were featured in virtually every muscle mag at one time or another.

The top five in the 1980 Ms. America contest included Carla Dunlap, Claudia Wilbourn, Lisa Elliott, Kay Baxter, and

fundamentals of women's bodybuilding

myself—all true women bodybuilders with fully developed muscles, symmetrical physiques, and tremendous cuts. As I stood onstage posing down against these four terrific bodybuilders, I felt that my quest for bodybuilding perfection had finally been actualized both in my own physique and in terms of the sport as a whole.

At the 1980 U.S. Championships, Laura had already developed plenty of muscle, but she had not yet learned how to train and diet for the sharp cuts that would win her the Ms. America title six months later. *(Bill Reynolds)*

Since the 1980 America, however, women's bodybuilding judging has entered a period of utter confusion. On one hand we have the "lovelies" who win high-level contests from time to time with minimal muscular development. On the other hand, we have a dedicated cadre of true female bodybuilders who are frequently discriminated against in many competitions.

As I—and numerous others—see it, women's bodybuilding can go in only one direction. As in men's bodybuilding we *must* go with the type of physique that is most difficult to achieve. Such a physique combines ideal symmetry and physical proportions, maximum muscular development, and diamond-hard muscularity. And *that* is the name of the game!

THE SPORT AND YOU

Thankfully, and despite the confusion in women's bodybuilding judging standards, thousands of women are flocking to the sport. The myths which used to discourage women from training with weights are dead. No one is gullible enough today to believe that bodybuilding training will make a woman muscle-bound or unfeminine. And as a result, women in all walks of life are flocking into gyms to train for bodybuilding competition.

How many women are currently competing in bodybuilding, or are interested in competing? I can best answer such questions—as well as document the explosive growth of the sport—with data provided to me by the editors of *Muscle & Fitness* magazine, the bible of bodybuilding. Each year *Muscle & Fitness* conducts a demographic survey of its readers. Table 1 (page 13) indicates an increase in female readership of the magazine of approximately 30 times the original figure between 1979 and 1982. Table 2 (page 13) indicates an increase between 1979 and 1982 in contests by a factor of 90, and in actual contestants by a factor of 100!

Quite obviously, women's bodybuilding is exploding in popularity, and its growth appears to be exponential. But, is it safe for a woman to train hard with heavy weights? Can a woman safely train as hard as a man can?

fundamentals of women's bodybuilding

Table 1: Readership Breakdown (Monthly)

Year	Total Copies Sold	Percentage Women Readers	Total Women Readers
1979	120,000	2½%	3,125
1980	185,000	8%	14,800
1981	260,000	19%	49,400
1982*	335,000	26%	87,100

*All 1982 figures are accurate as of June 1982.

Table 2: Women Competitors (Estimated)

Year	Total Competitions	Total Competitors
1979	2	30
1980	15	150
1981	80	800
1982*	180	3000

*Figures for 1982 are extrapolated for the full year on a basis of data for the first six months of the year.

Physiologically, heavy weight training is not harmful to a woman in normal health. And many women will be surprised to learn that we can actually train *harder* than men. Because men secrete the muscle-building hormone testosterone in huge quantities when compared to women, they will always be stronger and have larger muscles. But women *can* develop considerable strength and muscle mass. And women can become *much* more muscularly massive than anything we have seen so far in the sport.

While women will always be smaller and weaker than men in a workout, Nature has given women superior innate stamina and higher thresholds of pain than men have. Therefore—while we can't handle a man's training poundages—we *can* train at a higher level of intensity (which causes considerable pain from accumulated fatigue toxins) and for a longer period of time. Training with poundages relative to our own strength levels, we can literally waste virtually any male bodybuilder in a long, high-intensity workout. And *that* is a physiological fact!

HOW TRAINING WORKS

Hypertrophy is the scientific word for the process in which a muscle grows in mass and strength, and a muscle undergoes hypertrophy when it is stressed by a load heavier than it is used to handling. Physiologists summarize this concept by stating that an overload on a muscle leads to hypertrophy of that muscle.

As a muscle grows in mass and strength, however, it must be stressed with a heavier and heavier overload if it is to continue to hypertrophy. This is why we have progression of resistance in bodybuilding training. Without it, a woman bodybuilder's muscles would never reach an appropriate mass for competitive

"I feel that winning the Ms. America title vindicated my belief that women bodybuilders should have muscles, and *big* ones!" (Bill Heimanson)

fundamentals of women's bodybuilding

success. They would only become large and strong enough to handle the initial degree of overload.

Heavy weight training, therefore, is fundamental to successful bodybuilding. For optimum muscle hypertrophy, however, training must be accompanied by a healthy diet and a proper mental attitude toward bodybuilding preparation. A bodybuilder's diet is discussed in Chapter 3, plus synthesized in my own training philosophy in Chapter 11. A bodybuilder's mental attitude is discussed in greater detail in Chapters 10 and 11.

Bodybuilding, then, has three legs—much like the legs of a tripod—and it cannot stand if one of the three legs is weak or entirely missing. To achieve maximum muscle hypertrophy, you must combine hard training with a healthy diet and optimum mental attitude. Underplay any one of these factors, however, and you will fail to succeed in your quest to become a champion bodybuilder. You will read in detail how I personally combine these three legs of the "bodybuilding tripod" in my own training philosophy in Chapter 11.

TRAINING OPTIONS

When, where, and how you train are individual matters which must be determined by each woman. I have literally trained successfully at every time of day, even in the middle of the night. I'm convinced that the time of day you work out has little or nothing to do with bodybuilding success, as long as you *do* work out on a regular basis.

I personally train at home and in a number of organized gyms. It's great to play with the huge variety of equipment at Gold's Gym in Venice, California, but I've gotten equally good workouts training at home alone in my garage. So, as long as you are motivated to succeed, you will do so training *anywhere*.

How to train is another question, because individual bodies react differently to each training technique. What works well for me won't necessarily work equally well for, say, Lisa Elliott, or for you. You must experiment with every possible training technique and routine, using your training "instinct" (discussed in detail in Chapter 9) to determine what works best on your unique body. Every champion woman bodybuilder has done this, so you aren't alone in your quest.

In the final analysis, it doesn't matter when, where, or (to some degree) how you train as long as you *do* train. Just get into the gym and pump iron. And if you don't have time to train, make the time!

THE BODYBUILDING LIFESTYLE

I'm not going to lie to you—the life of a serious competitive bodybuilder is not an easy one. Bodybuilding is the world's toughest sport, since we are forced to train for long hours while dieting quite strictly. It takes a rare breed of woman to become a champion bodybuilder. Getting into peak condition is a full-time job for me. I personally devote 8–10 hours a day to my bodybuilding workouts, aerobic training sessions, posing practice, psychological preparation, and sunbathing. Without such total commitment to my sport, I would never have won the Ms. America title.

For all champions in our sport, bodybuilding is a way of life. As in any other sport, a champion bodybuilder must make training and other facets of contest preparation the number one priority in her life. A missed workout can never be made up. *You* and only you can train and diet intensely enough to become a winner. No one else can do it for you.

Therefore, if you are to become a champion woman bodybuilder you must first decide if it is worth the effort to you. Then you must make a firm commitment to reach that goal. Finally, you must establish a lifestyle in which bodybuilding takes first priority. This means that you must sacrifice much of your social life, many of the foods you prefer to eat, and numerous other minor pleasures that the seething masses enjoy. In a word, you must be dedicated to the sport. But I'm sure that you *are* that special breed of woman who will thrive on a lifestyle of self-sacrifice, dedication, and ultimate victory.

fundamentals of women's bodybuilding

"The lifestyle of a competitive bodybuilder is extremely disciplined, so an occasional moment of relaxation from training, dieting, posing, and sunning is always welcome." *(Bill Dobbins)*

To maintain a successful bodybuilding lifestyle you must set realistic goals. These goals should be both long-term and short-term in nature. Long-term goals are usually set for a lifetime, or perhaps for one-year periods of time, and they are grand in scope. Typical examples of long-term goals are to win your state title, to win the Miss Olympia title, to be using 25 pounds more on your Bench Press poundage, or to add an inch to your upper arm girth.

Since long-term goals tend to be somewhat mindboggling, they should be broken up into numerous, more achievable, short-term goals covering one-week or one-month time periods. As an example of a short-term goal, you need increase your Bench Press poundage by less than 2½ pounds per month to achieve a long-term goal of adding 25 pounds to your exercise weight for that movement in one year. It's much easier for your mind to conceive of adding 2½ pounds (a short-term goal) to your Bench Press workout poundage than to add 25 pounds to it. But, 12 months of adding 2½ pounds per month actually adds up to a 30-pound increase!

Personally, my long-term goal is to achieve an image of my physique that I have developed and mentally visualized over the years. And it will no doubt take me several more years to achieve this goal, to actualize the visualized image. But, you can rest assured that I will one day reach this long-term goal.

Although I had once set Bench Pressing 200 pounds as a short-term goal, my usual short-term goals are set more in terms of seeing noticeable improvement in each underpar muscle group than in terms of using certain exercise poundages. I'll pick one or two such body parts each couple of months and really concentrate hard on bringing them up. Gradually and steadily bringing up such weaknesses—one after the other—will eventually bring me to my long-term goal of actualizing my image of ultimate personal physical development.

FEMALE FACTORS IN BODYBUILDING

Such factors as menstruation, amenorrhea, pregnancy and childbirth, menopause, and, to a degree, birth control are unique to female bodybuilders. Menopause is no doubt inapplicable to most competitive bodybuilders, but you can rest assured that the regular exercise and healthy diet of a bodybuilder's lifestyle will minimize menopausal difficulties. In societies which keep women physically active, menopausal difficulties are virtually unknown.

Women who experience menstrual cramps and other ills will soon find them a thing of the past once they are fully into a bodybuilding lifestyle. Many female bodybuilders—as well as other women athletes—do experience amenorrhea (a cessation of menstrual periods), however.

While amenorrhea is distressing to many poorly informed women, scientific studies have indicated that it causes no harm to a female athlete's health or reproductive system. Amenorrhea

fundamentals of women's bodybuilding

appears to be related to body fat level. Women below a body fat level constituting approximately 10 percent of body weight experience amenorrhea, but once body fat is allowed to climb above 10 percent, normal menstrual function is resumed.

There is some debate over whether a woman ovulates when amenorrheic. Until it has been firmly established that all amenorrheic women cease to ovulate, amenorrhea should be treated as a very unreliable method of birth control!

A woman bodybuilder needn't fear becoming pregnant, since numerous champions were either mothers prior to commencing bodybuilding training or were able to quickly regain top condition after giving birth. Auby Paulik, the sensation of the 1980 Miss Olympia competition, for example, gave birth in 1981 and was back in peak condition—complete with her accustomed super-sharp abdominal development—in 1982. And, incidentally, the bodybuilding lifestyle minimizes pregnancy and delivery complications, results in shorter and easier labor, and allows a woman to regain more quickly superb physical condition following childbirth.

To sexually active women bodybuilders who don't desire to become pregnant, birth control is an important issue. And if your lover won't take responsibility for contraception, you must intelligently choose a safe and convenient method of birth control. For serious women bodybuilders, birth control pills are definitely out. The estrogen and progesterone in them results in considerable water retention within the body. There is even evidence that these hormones will reduce muscle mass. And, birth control pills are not without other, more serious side effects. One of my friends, a superb rugby player, was seriously disabled as a result of a brain hemorrhage related to taking birth control pills.

I've polled numerous top women bodybuilders on the topic of birth control. A majority of sexually active champion women bodybuilders prefer to use a diaphragm for contraception. Correctly fitted and used, a diaphragm is a safe and effective contraceptive device which can have no deleterious effect on your progress as a competitive bodybuilder.

Photo by Mike Neveux.

chapter three
intermediate techniques

In this chapter I will discuss the use of a training partner and a bodybuilding diary, how to develop training instinct, basic diet tips, and what bodybuilding potential means to you. Master these techniques and concepts, and you will be well on your way to becoming a winning woman bodybuilder.

TRAINING PARTNERS

I have trained successfully both with a partner and by myself. If you can find a partner who has similar goals and an attitude toward training that's the same as your own, then you should train with that person. Otherwise, I feel that you're better off training alone.

Richard Baldwin and Laura trained together at Gold's Gym (as in the above picture) and at his Body Forum gym in Tallahassee for the 1980 American Championships. Both of them won their titles, which was a tremendous source of self-satisfaction.

intermediate techniques

I've had a couple of training partners in the past whom I felt I was always pulling through a workout, so I abandoned them. A partnership should be a partnership. Both partners should benefit from it, or it should be dissolved. A training partner should motivate you and you should motivate your partner. You can't be up for every workout and neither can your training partner, so you have a responsibility to each other to share energies and push harder than usual when the other person is a little down in energy and training drive.

Without a doubt, the best training partner I've ever had was Richard Baldwin, whom I mentioned in the previous chapter. As a result, I am very much in favor of male-female training partnerships, as long as you can keep your relationship confined to the gym. There's often too much competitiveness between two women who train together, and this is eliminated in male-female partnerships.

You will also find that a man's and woman's respective physiological makeup complement each other. We aren't as strong as men, so they tend to inspire us by example to lift heavier weights in our workouts. On the other hand, we generally have greater endurance than men, which allows us to inspire them to train harder and longer each workout day.

TRAINING DIARIES

It's essential that you maintain an accurate training and nutrition diary over the years. With an accurate and detailed diary, you can look back and see how much you have improved over the months and years you have been training. Over a week or so, it's difficult to see noticeable improvement in your training poundages. From year to year, however, such increases are dramatically evident. Therefore, your diary can be a great source of inspiration to you whenever you are feeling a little down.

Even more important, a bodybuilding log is the only sure way you can keep tabs on how your training, diet, and emotional well-being affect your muscle gain rate. Without a diary, you'll just be guessing at how well you are progressing. A training diary is probably the best way to develop the training instinct needed to make sense of the experiments you make in your training routines and diet.

Your bodybuilding log should cover as much detail as possible. You can use abbreviations if you like, as long as they are intelligible to you. Any notebook or bound ledger book will be okay for keeping detailed diary entries, or you can buy an inexpensive, professionally produced training log in book stores. It is put out by *Muscle & Fitness* magazine and Contemporary Books, Inc., the publisher of this book. It is called *Joe Weider's* Muscle & Fitness *Training Diary*.

One practice I use in my own diaries is to include photographs of myself taken at one-month intervals (you can simply glue or

Laura records her daily workouts.

intermediate techniques

tape them to a page of the diary). These photos not only reveal how much new muscle mass I am adding, but also the shape, quality and proportional balance of that muscle tissue over the years. And by reviewing the relative body fat levels—which are readily apparent in these photos—I can make conclusions about which dietary practices are leading to the best degree of contest muscularity.

TRAINING INSTINCT

All champion bodybuilders have a highly developed bodybuilding instinct that allows them to "feel," within a very short time, whether a new exercise, workout program, training technique, or dietary variation will be valuable to them. With some bodybuilding variables, I can personally tell almost immediately if they are of any value. Other variables may require a week or so of experimentation and "feel" to evaluate.

Most bodybuilders are constantly searching for new techniques that will help them to reach the top. It's almost like a scientific experiment with your body as the lab. If you are less experienced as a bodybuilder, your training diary will be your best friend in determining the value of new techniques. But as you become more experienced and refine your training instinct, this instinct will greatly shorten the amount of time it can take to determine relative values. As such, training instinct is one of a bodybuilder's most valuable tools.

So, how do you go about developing this training instinct? Primarily, you should learn to listen to the biofeedback signals that your body gives you every day. As an example, a good muscle pump is one way in which to determine that you have had an optimum workout for a particular body part.

Read the following questions and try to answer them. What would chronic fatigue tell you? Sore muscles the day after a particular workout? A growing accumulation of body fat? Inability to sleep soundly? A painful knee? An added inch of muscle girth in your upper arm?

Chronic fatigue tells you that you are either overtraining or not sleeping enough. Sore muscles tell you that the workout you did a day or two ago was more intense than what your muscles have been used to handling. A growing accumulation of body fat indicates that your diet is too high in calories. Insomnia or fitful sleep is a sure sign of overtraining. A painful knee is usually injured. And added muscle mass in any body part indicates that you are progressing well in your training and diet.

The above is just a sampling of the biofeedback signals your body gives you. There are scores more that you should gradually learn to monitor. And with time and experience, these signals will help you to develop the type of training instinct that all champion bodybuilders have acquired. If you are a relatively inexperienced bodybuilder, this may be a little difficult to believe, but all of the champions have gone through the process I have just described.

DIET TIPS

Some bodybuilders feel that diet is 75%-80% of the battle in bodybuilding. I wouldn't put the figure quite that high, but certainly up to 50% of my own bodybuilding success, particularly just prior to a contest, is a result of proper dietary practices. Therefore, it's important to understand why you should eat various foods as a bodybuilder.

Proper nutrition is absolutely essential if you hope to get the most out of your bodybuilding training. Varying qualities of food in the human body gives you essentially the same results energy-wise, and in terms of muscle-building ability, as varying qualities of gasoline in an automobile. Use a poor quality of food or an inferior octane gas, and the body or car runs poorly. But if you use food or gasoline of good quality, they both run well.

Protein

For active athletes and bodybuilders, protein is one of the most important dietary elements. Protein is necessary for optimum muscle mass growth and strength increase, as well as for tissue

intermediate techniques

repair throughout the body. The best sources of proteins are lean meats, poultry, fish, eggs, and milk products.

You should obtain a book that lists the nutrient contents of various foods (the *Nutrition Almanac*, McGraw-Hill, 1979, is ideal). Get into the habit of calculating how much protein—as well as how much of each other food element—you consume each day. And you can summarize these nutrient values every day in your bodybuilding diary.

The U.S. Food and Drug Administration has set one gram per kilogram (2.2 pounds) of body weight—or a little less than one-half gram per pound—as the Adult Minimum Daily Requirement (AMDR) of protein. My opinion is that a half gram of protein per pound of body weight is about enough for the average sedentary chipmunk. An active bodybuilder requires one gram (and perhaps even more) of protein per pound of body weight. Do you want to be a chipmunk or a pumper? In terms of protein intake, the choice is yours!

Fats

A certain degree of fat intake is necessary for healthy biological function, but be careful about how much fat you consume each day. When broken down in the human body for energy, or for energy storage in the form of body fat, fat yields nine calories per gram, versus four calories per gram for both protein and carbohydrate. Therefore, fats are more than twice as concentrated a source of energy as protein and carbs, and they should be limited in a serious bodybuilder's diet.

My own diet is low in fat year-round, and particularly so prior to a competition when I am trying to get really cut up. A major share of the fats that I do consume are polyunsaturated, meaning they come from vegetable sources and have not been chemically hydrogenated to harden the fat. Polyunsaturated fats contain lipotropics, which help you to lose body fat when on a tight precontest diet.

Keep in mind that you will need to consume at least a little fat each day, or you will be unable to assimilate the fat-soluble vitamins (A, D, E, K, and P).

Carbohydrates

Carbohydrates are the body's favorite source of energy fuel. While fats are broken down slowly for energy in the body, carbohydrate foods are a quick source of energy. The best sources of carbohydrates are fresh fruits, fresh vegetables, whole grains (especially rice), and potatoes. You should always strive to avoid refined carbohydrates found in white sugar, flour, and alcohol.

I have a moderate intake of carbohydrates year-round, except for a short period of time just prior to competing when I virtually eliminate carbohydrate consumption. Carbohydrates retain four times their weight in water in the body, and eliminating them prior to competing flushes water from my body, making my skin look very tight over my muscles.

Fiber

Fiber is often called "roughage" these days, and many high-fiber diets have been suggested to improve health. Fiber is merely the indigestible cellulose part of fruits, vegetables, nuts, and grains. It gives bulk to the stool, and is a vital part of any healthy diet. In order to consume fiber, try to have at least one serving of fresh fruit (particularly pears) and one of fresh green vegetables (lettuce, celery, green beans, etc.) each day.

Vitamins and Minerals

Fresh foods supply many of the vitamins and minerals you need for proper body function and optimum health. Processed foods have had most of the vitamins and minerals leached out and replaced by poor synthetic substitutes. Therefore, you have another good reason to eat fresh foods and avoid junk foods.

Ordinarily, the contents of one or two "multi-packs" of vitamins and minerals per day are sufficient nutritional insurance against vitamin and mineral deficiencies. However, close to a competition, when your diet is ordinarily quite restricted, you will no doubt require a great deal more supplementation.

intermediate techniques

Vitamin and mineral deficiencies will slow your progress as a bodybuilder, and they can be very insidious. Many such deficiencies of water-soluble vitamins and minerals (like B-complex vitamins and potassium) show up quickly and can be corrected easily. If you consistently feel weak and lack energy during your workouts, for example, you are probably deficient in B-complex and potassium, if not also in other vitamins and minerals.

Water

Depending on how much you perspire as you train, you will need to drink at least 7–10 glasses of water and other fluids every day. In addition to perspiration losses of water, you will also release considerable water vapor with each breath you expel.

Taking in too little fluid will dehydrate your body, which often results in weakness, lack of energy, and painful muscle cramps. So, go ahead and drink water whenever you feel thirsty, even if it's in the middle of a workout. With all of the impurities and chemicals in metropolitan water supplies, I feel that most city dwellers would be better off drinking bottled water.

Weight-Loss Dieting

To lose fat weight, you must create a caloric deficit. In other words, you must consume less calories in your food each day than you use up in your daily activities and bodily metabolic processes. And with each accumulated deficit of 3,500 calories, you will lose one pound of body fat.

The best way to reduce caloric consumption is to cut back on the amount of fats you eat. And to reduce fats, you need merely cut gradually back on the amount of red meat you might eat, replacing it ounce for ounce with white meats like fish, chicken, and turkey. Beef and pork are quite high in fats, while the white meats are relatively low. Eating more protein and carbs, and less fat, significantly reduces the number of calories you are receiving, hence, allowing you to reduce your fatty body weight.

I have found that staying just a little hungry at all times is essential if I wish to reduce my body fat levels. Eat small quantities of food only when you are truly hungry, eat slowly, and stop eating before your appetite is completely satiated. And, *never* eat any refined or processed foods when you are trying to reduce your body's fat levels.

Weight-Gain Dieting

To gain muscular body weight, you will need to train very heavy and consume an excess of calories in your diet, preferably with the excess calories made up of muscle-building protein foods. To do this, I suggest eating a fairly well-balanced diet, weighted a little more toward protein foods.

You should also try eating five or six small meals each day rather than three large ones. Your body can only digest and assimilate approximately 20–25 grams of protein per feeding, so more frequent meals augment the amount of protein your body uses. This keeps you constantly in a positive nitrogen balance, which is a requisite for fast growth in muscle mass. And, be sure to take enough vitamin and mineral supplements to prevent progress-halting nutritional deficiencies.

Here is a one-day menu for weight-gain dieting that will help you to pack on muscle mass as quickly as possible:

Meal 1—7:00 a.m.
- 2–3 scrambled eggs
- piece of whole-grain toast
- serving of fruit
- glass of milk or cup of coffee
- food supplements

Meal 2—10:00 a.m.
- tuna salad made with one can of water-packed tuna, 1½–2 tablespoons of safflower mayonnaise, diced pickle, onion, and celery
- glass of milk

intermediate techniques

Meal 3—1:00 p.m.
- meat, poultry, or fish entree
- 1-2 vegetables or a salad
- iced tea
- food supplements

Meal 4—4:00 p.m.
- 3 ounces of hard cheese
- piece of fruit
- glass of milk or vegetable juice

Meal 5—7:00 p.m.
- poultry or fish entree
- serving of rice or potatoes
- 1-2 vegetable servings
- glass of milk or a cup of coffee
- food supplements

Meal 6—10:00 p.m.
- cup of yogurt with fresh fruit or 2-3 hard-boiled eggs
- glass of milk or vegetable juice

For one or more of these meals—particularly when you are so rushed that you might ordinarily have missed a meal—you can substitute in a protein shake. Using a blender, mix up the following ingredients:

- 8-10 ounces of milk or juice
- 2 tablespoons of milk and egg protein powder
- 1-2 pieces of soft fruit (e.g., peaches, bananas, or pears) for flavoring if desired

Blended well and served cold, this makes a taste-pleasing and highly nutritious milkshake.

You can play with the suggested order and timing of the meals to suit your work/school and workout schedules, and you can vary the quantities of foods according to your appetite. You can also experiment with different foods within the general outline provided, but be sure to avoid junk foods.

Eliminate from your weight-gaining diet all salt, white sugar, baked goods, soft drinks, alcoholic beverages, prepared foods, and fake juice drinks. These so-called foods will definitely add weight to your body, but it will be 100% useless fat.

BODYBUILDING POTENTIAL

Much has been written about genetic potential for bodybuilding and about how only very gifted athletes can hope to become champions in our sport. I strongly disagree with this contention, preferring to consider genetic potential to be an enabling factor rather than a limiting factor. More simply put, certain genetic advantages will allow you to reach your goals more quickly, but there are few (if any) genetic disadvantages that will keep you

intermediate techniques

from becoming a viable competitive bodybuilder if you have enough desire and are willing to pay the price in your diet and training programs.

In bodybuilding, proof of the pudding lies in what you do with your genetic potential, regardless of how good or bad it might be. There are no excuses in our sport for undertraining, missing workouts, or failing to follow a healthy diet, and the worst excuse of all is your perception that you might not have great potential. Work with what God and your parents have given you, because poor heredity is a factor that *can* be overcome in women's bodybuilding.

Heredity becomes a crucial factor only when you begin to approach your ultimate potential. However, you should bear in mind that no woman bodybuilder—nor any male bodybuilder, for that matter—has even begun to approach her ultimate physical potential. Perhaps you will become the first to do so.

Photo by Mike Neveux.

chapter four
chest exercises

The chest muscle complex consists entirely of the pectoral muscles which act to pull the upper arm bones directly forward, forward and upward simultaneously, or forward and downward simultaneously. Male bodybuilders tend to work their lower pecs quite hard, but a woman's breasts and posing attire cover this area. Therefore, you will be more or less wasting your time doing lower-pec exercises like Parallel Bar Dips, Decline Presses, and Decline Flyes. It's better for a woman to work hard on the upper and middle pectoral areas, since they are the parts of your chest that can be seen onstage at a competition.

BENCH PRESS

This is the most basic of all chest movements. It strongly stresses the whole pectoral muscle, the front deltoids, and the triceps muscles. I take a grip on the bar 4–6 inches wider on each side than the width of my shoulders. Then I make sure I am lying solidly on the bench and take the weight off the rack to straight arms' length above my shoulder joints. As I lower the barbell down to touch my upper chest, I am very careful to be sure that my upper arm bones travel directly out to the sides and perpendicular to my torso. A mistake many novice bodybuilders make is allowing their elbows to travel more toward their feet, which takes considerable stress off the pectorals. I am very careful to avoid bouncing the bar off my chest before pushing it back to the starting point.

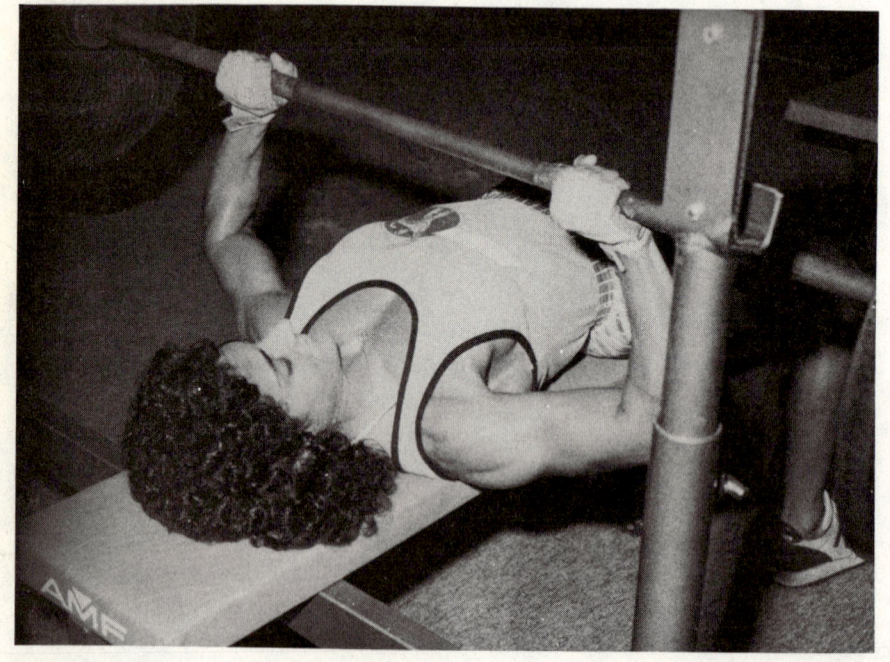

Bench Press.

When doing very heavy Benches it's important to have a spotter standing at the head end of the bench to rescue you if you get stuck at the bottom of a rep or start to pass out from the exertion of the movement.

Incline Barbell Press.

INCLINE BARBELL PRESS

This is a key movement for building mass in the upper sections of your pectorals. Inclines also strongly stress the front deltoids and triceps. I take the same grip on a barbell as for Bench Presses and lift the bar off the rack into a position where it is at straight arms' length directly above my shoulder joints. Then I lower the barbell slowly and directly downward to lightly touch my upper chest at the base of my neck. For the most direct upper pectoral stimulation, you *must* keep your elbows back as you lower the weight and then press it back to the starting position. Again, a spotter is important when you are using maximum poundages. I prefer a bench set at a 45-degree angle for all incline movements.

FLAT-BENCH/INCLINE FLYES

Flat-Bench Flyes stress the whole pectoral mass, while Incline Flyes transfer stress more to the upper pecs. I do both movements from time to time. Regardless of the bench I use, I keep my palms

Flat-Bench Flyes.

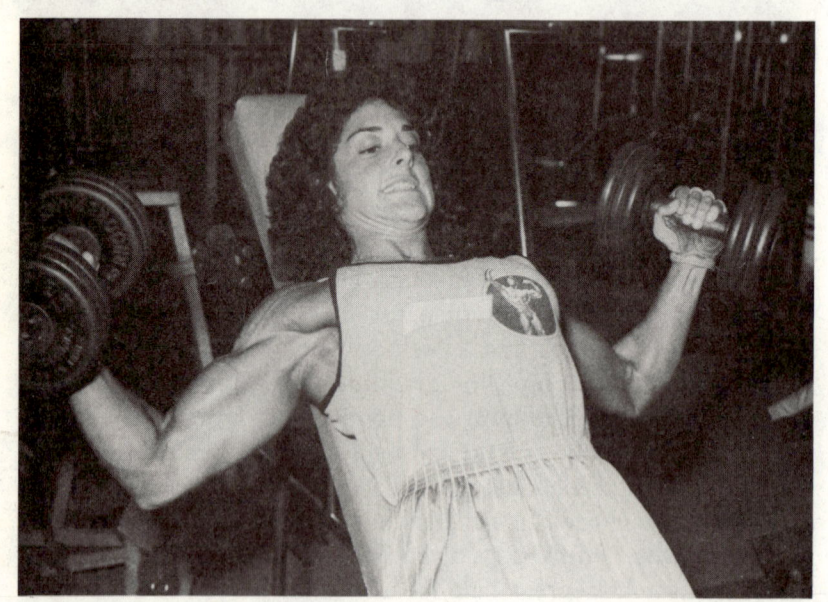

Incline Flyes.

facing each other (or facing upward in the low position of the exercise) throughout the movement. As with the foregoing pressing movements, the key to using Flyes effectively is to keep your elbows back as you do the movement. I also keep my arms slightly bent to keep stress off my elbows. The further you can

chest exercises

lower your elbows below the level of your chest on this exercise, the higher the quality of stress you place on your pecs.

CROSS-BENCH PULLOVERS

This exercise stresses the entire pectoral muscle, as well as the impressive serratus muscles at the sides of your rib cage. With lighter weights—and in combination with Breathing Squats—these Pullovers will help you to enlarge the volume of your rib

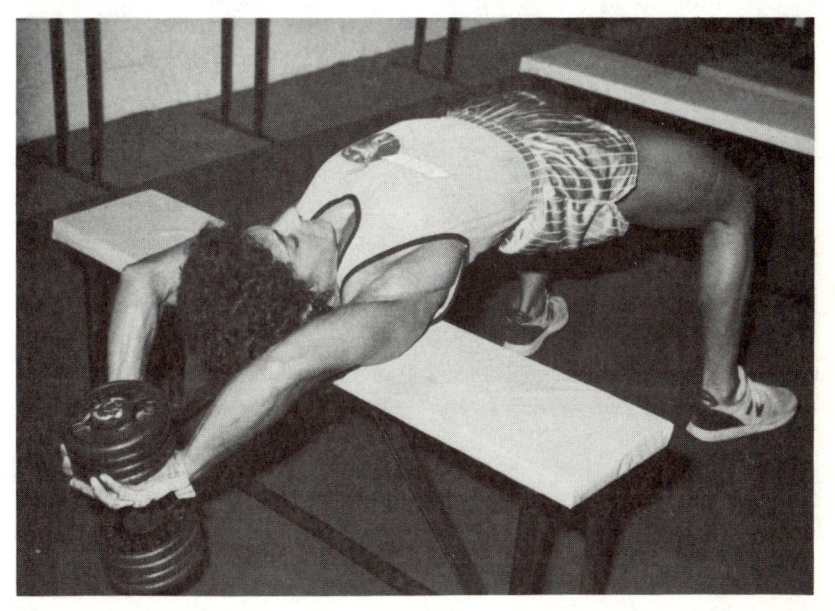

Cross-Bench Pullover.

box. I lay a heavy dumbbell on end on the top of a flat exercise bench and then position my shoulders and upper back across the bench next to the dumbbell. After placing my feet in a balanced position, I grasp the dumbbell with my palms flat against the inside top plate and with my thumbs around the dumbbell handle. Then I swing the weight into the starting position, which is at straight arms' length above my chest. From that position, I simultaneously lower the weight backward and dowward in a semicircle while bending my arms a bit. You will get more stretch in your chest muscles if you also lower your hips as you lower the weight. Then I return the dumbbell to the starting position and repeat the movement.

Cable Crossover.

CABLE CROSSOVERS

This is an excellent movement for bringing out the striations across your pectorals, particularly along the groove that separates your pectoral muscles along your sternum. I grasp the two pulley handles and am careful to keep my palms downward throughout the movement. Then I bend forward at the waist so my torso is at about a 45-degree angle with the floor. Then after allowing my hands to travel upward as high as possible, I bend my arms slightly and pull the handles in semicircles until they meet directly in front of my hips. Next, I tense my pecs and delts hard in this position, much like when doing a most-muscular pose in a contest. Then I slowly return the handles to the starting position.

chest exercises

PEC DECK FLYES

This is an excellent overall pectoral developer, but I do it specifically to add mass and cuts to my inner pecs where they meet at the sternum. I've never found an exercise to equal Pec Deck Flyes for that purpose. Adjust the seat of the machine so your upper arms are approximately parallel to the floor as your forearms run up the pads and your fingertips curl over the tops of the movable pads. I stretch my pecs by allowing the pads to travel backward as far as possible. Then I slowly force the pads forward until they touch each other in front of my chest. For a peak contraction effect, you can hold the pads together for a count of two or three before returning them to the starting position. By moving the seat upward or downward a little you can feel the movement differently and hit your pecs from a greater variety of angles.

GENERAL COMMENTS

Most pectoral exercises involve the front deltoids to a degree, a few of them quite strongly. You won't be able to isolate your delts from the movements, but you can keep them from bearing a disproportionate amount of the load in an exercise by strongly concentrating your mind on the working pectorals. Feel and visualize your pecs extending and contracting under resistance, and the effect of your delts on a chest movement will be minimized.

Photo by Bill Reynolds.

chapter five
back exercises

Your back consists of three major muscle groups. The trapezius muscles of the upper back contract to pull your shoulders upward and backward. The erector spinae muscles of your lower back contract to straighten your body from a position where it is bent at the waist. And your latissimus dorsi muscles contract to pull your upper arms backward and downward.

There are two basic types of lat movements and each serves a different function. Rowing movements, such as Barbell Bent Rows and Seated Pulley Rowing, add thickness to your lats and upper back muscles. Pulldown movements, such as Chins and Lat Pulldowns, add width to your lats. It is also important for you to know that you will receive a much better contraction in your lats when you do each movement with your spine arched.

Barbell Bent Row.

BARBELL BENT ROWING

I consider this exercise to be the basic movement for lat development. It also secondarily stresses the lower back muscles, trapezius and biceps. I take a shoulder-width grip on the bar, bend over until my torso is parallel to the floor and slightly unlock my knees to take stress off my lower back. Then I pull the barbell up to touch the bottom part of my chest, being sure that my upper arm bones travel outward away from my torso at approximately 45-degree angles on each side. When I lower the bar back down, I try to stretch my lats at the bottom of the movement. If you find that the barbell plates touch the floor before you reach a fully stretched position, either stand on a thick block of wood when you do the movement or use plates with a smaller diameter.

T-Bar Row.

T-BAR ROWING

This is a very good movement for lat and lower back thickness. There are several variations of T-bars, some that use plates and some that use a pulley. There also are a variety of handles you can use, some with parallel grips and some with a straight bar welded across the main movement bar. I bend my knees a little again, try to get a good stretch at the bottom and pull the weight up until it touches my chest. My torso rocks back and forth a little more on this movement than on Barbell Bent Rows. If you use plates with a smaller diameter, you will find that you can both lower them down further and pull your hands closer to your chest at the top of the movement.

WIDE-GRIP CHINS

This is my basic lat width movement. I take a grip on the bar so my hands are set at least 6–8 inches wider on each side than the width of my shoulders. For balance, I bend my legs and cross my ankles behind me. Then, with an arched back, I slowly pull myself up until my upper chest touches the bar. From that position, I slowly lower my body down to the starting position, being sure to stretch my lats at the bottom by fully straightening my arms. You also can do these chins to the back of your neck, but I feel I get more out of them when I do them to the front of my neck.

LAT PULLDOWNS

This is another good lat movement, and it's especially good if you still lack the strength to do at least five or six good Chins. I do two versions. In the first, I take a wide grip on the bar, arch my back and pull the bar down to touch my trapezius behind my neck. On the second version, I take a narrow reversed grip and pull the bar down as far as I can along the front of my body. The wide-grip version hits my upper lats quite hard, while the narrow-grip variation seems to stress my lower lats more.

Lat Pulldown.

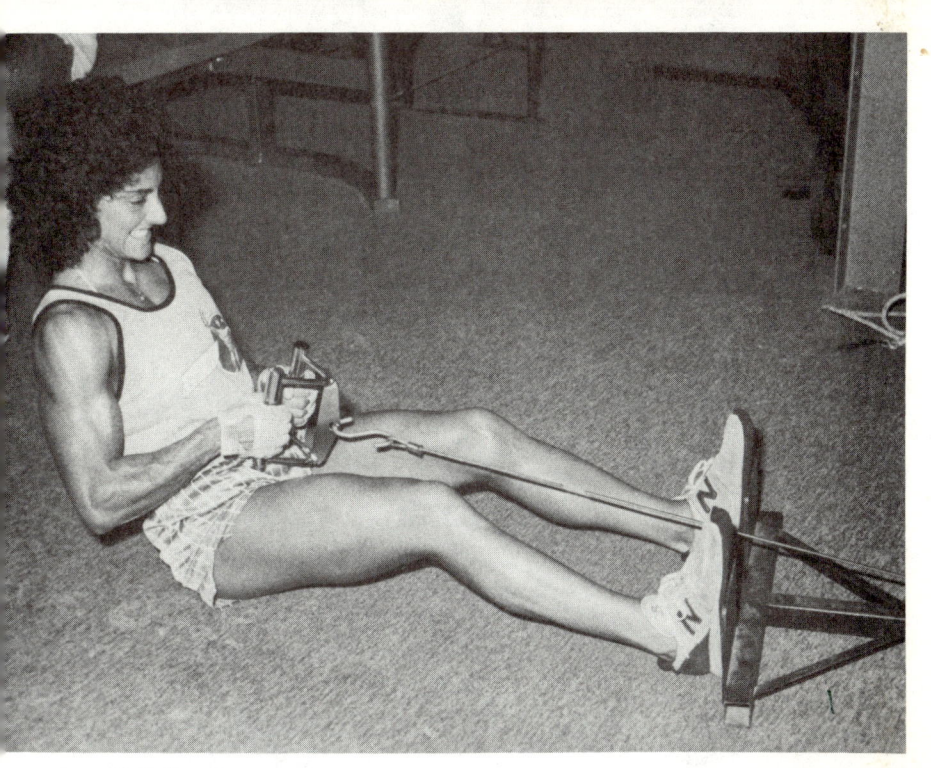

Seated Pulley Row.

SEATED PULLEY ROWING

As with T-Bar Rowing, there are several types of handles you can use on this machine. While some bodybuilders perfer to use a straight-bar handle, I like the one which allows me to take a narrow grip with my palms facing each other. I bend my legs a little, fully straighten my arms and lean toward the pulley to completely stretch my lats at the beginning of the movement. To stretch your lats even more fully, you can drop your head between your arms. From this position, I simultaneously sit upright, arch my back, and pull the pulley handle in to touch my upper abdomen. I am sure to pull my upper arms both backward and a little downward as I pull the bar in. Then I return to the starting position and repeat the movement for the desired number of reps. In my experience, Seated Pulley Rowing tends to build lat width *and* lat thickness, so it is a key exercise with most top bodybuilders.

One-Arm Cable Row.

ONE-ARM CABLE ROWING

You'll find this to be a good finishing-off movement to any lat routine. Some bodybuilders like to do the rows one arm at a time while facing the floor pulley and standing in a crouch. I personally prefer to have the cable pass across the front of my body and do the movement in the same fashion you would pull the cord that starts a lawn mower. I do go for a complete stretch at the beginning of the movement and fully contract my lats at the completion of the exercise. I've tried doing One-Arm Pulley Rows with a high pulley, too, and it seems to hit them beneficially, although from a slightly different angle. On all one-arm exercises, you will find that you can concentrate on the movement more completely than when doing the same exercise with both arms.

back exercises

GENERAL COMMENTS

You will notice that I haven't included in this chapter any direct movements for the trapezius or lower back muscles. I do Upright Rows as part of my deltoid program (see Chapter 6) and this exercise gives me sufficient trapezius stimulation. If your own traps tend to lag behind, you may have to do Barbell or Dumbbell Shrugs. You can also do Shrugs quite conveniently using the Bench Press station on a Universal Gym machine.

My lower back has developed quite well as a result of the stress placed on my lumbar muscles when I do various types of Bent Rows and Squats. If your lower back is lagging, however, include in your routine a few sets of Hyperextensions while holding a light barbell plate behind your head. This will very quickly bring up your erector spinae muscles.

Photo by Bill Dobbins.

chapter six
shoulder exercises

Although some bodybuilders consider the trapezius muscles of the upper back to be a part of the shoulder complex, I personally deal only with the deltoids in discussing shoulder development. The deltoid consists of three heads (or lobes)—the anterior (front) head, the medial (side) head and the posterior (rear) head. To fully develop your deltoid muscles, you must do specific training for each of these three heads.

The anterior deltoid head contracts to move the upper arm bone forward and upward. With your palm held forward or upward, it can also contract to move the upper arm to the side and upward. The medial deltoid head contracts to move the upper arm bone to the side and upward when the palm is held downward during the movement. And the posterior head of the deltoid contracts to move the upper arm bone directly to the rear.

Dumbbell Press.

DUMBBELL PRESS

I always do this exercise standing, and it's always the first movement in my routine. I only use Dumbbell Presses as a shoulder warmup. Of all the joints in your body, the shoulder is the weakest and most likely to be injured. Therefore, I am always careful to fully warm up my shoulder joints and muscles prior to commencing a heavy deltoid workout.

I hold the dumbbells throughout the movement with my palms forward, although as an alternative method of performance you can press dumbbells with your palms facing each other. Beginning with the inside plates of the dumbbells touching my deltoids, I slowly push them directly upward until my arms are straight and the dumbbells are touching in the middle directly above my head. I think it's important when you are warming up to do your Dumbbell Presses with a very slow cadence both upward and downward. And you certainly should never bounce the weights off your shoulders during the movement. Instead, raise and lower the dumbbells with full and deliberate control.

Military Press.

MILITARY PRESS

This is my heavy mass-building shoulder movement. On all heavy Overhead Pressing exercises I prefer to wear a lifting belt to protect my lower back from injury. I am also careful on all Overhead Pressing movements to stand as upright as possible. It's very easy to bend back and cheat up a heavier weight, but such a movement does little for the shoulders in a bodybuilding sense. I don't clean the bar for Military Presses, but instead take it off a squat rack after I've loaded it to the appropriate poundage. Once I have the weight at my shoulders, I lower my elbows so they are directly under the bar, and I keep them under the bar throughout the movement. Then it's simply a matter of pressing the barbell directly upward past your face until your arms are locked out straight and the barbell is directly above your head. Lower the barbell slowly back down until it touches your deltoids again before pressing it for a second rep.

Upright Row.

UPRIGHT ROWING

Some bodybuilders use a shoulder-width grip on this exercise. I've tried that grip on my Upright Rows, but I just can't feel the movement when I use that wide a grip. Therefore, I always do my Upright Rowing with a narrow grip (four or five inches between my index fingers). I stand erect with my arms straight and the barbell resting across my upper thighs. Then, always standing erect, I slowly bend my arms and pull the barbell upward along the front of my body until my hands touch the underside of my chin. Throughout the movement you should concentrate on keeping your elbows above the level of your hands, since this places maximum stress on your deltoids and trapezius muscles. Be sure to lower the barbell *slowly* back to the starting position before initiating another repetition. While I usually use a barbell for my Upright Rowing, you can also use a floor pulley. The pulley will actually give you a little better continuous tension effect than the barbell, but the movement generally feels a little awkward to me.

Dumbbell Side Lateral.

DUMBBELL SIDE LATERALS

Correctly performed, this exercise strongly stimulates the medial head of your deltoid. Grasp two light dumbbells in your hands and stand erect with your palms facing each other and the dumbbells touching about three or four inches in front of your hips. Your arms should be slightly bent throughout the movement. Bend slightly forward and maintain that position throughout the movement. From this basic starting position, slowly raise the dumbbells in semicircles from the position in front of your hips until they are at shoulder height. At the top of the movement, rotate your thumbs downward momentarily before you begin to lower the weights back to the starting point. This thumb rotation places very direct and very strong stress on the medial head of your deltoid.

DUMBBELL FRONT RAISE

You'll find that this movement very strongly stresses the anterior heads of your deltoids. A few bodybuilders do Front Raises with a barbell, but most of us do the exercise with two dumbbells,

Dumbbell Front Raise.

raising one as the other descends. Doing the movement in alternate style like this greatly lessens the chance of cheating by swinging the dumbbells upward. I start this movement with two light dumbbells resting on my thighs and my palms toward my thighs. My hands don't rotate at all during the movement. From this position I slowly raise one dumbbell upward to shoulder level, moving it more up the center line of my body rather than up a plane through my legs. Then, as that dumbbell begins to come down, I start to raise the other one. At times, I will raise the dumbbells all the way up to straight arms' length overhead.

Seated Bent Lateral.

SEATED BENT LATERALS

I always do my Bent Laterals seated, because I simply can't feel the movement as strongly when I do them standing. I sit at the end of a flat exercise bench with my feet on the floor in front of me. My feet will be set rather close together throughout the movement. Then I grasp two light dumbbells in my hands and bend forward until my torso is resting along the tops of my thighs. Keeping my arms slightly bent throughout the movement, I start with the dumbbells lightly touching each other beneath my thighs. Then I raise them directly out to the sides in semicircles until they are above the level of my shoulders. Be careful that you don't raise the dumbbells a little to the rear. If you err in any direction away from an angle at 90-degrees from your torso, it should be in raising the dumbbells a little to the front. All types of Bent Laterals strongly stress the posterior delts, and secondarily stress the upper back muscles.

Prone Incline Lateral.

PRONE INCLINE LATERALS

I like this exercise a lot because it strongly stresses both the medial and posterior heads of my deltoids, tying the two together and giving my shoulders a much more completely developed look than if I didn't do the movement. I lie facedown on a 45-degree incline bench with two dumbbells held in my hands. I bend my arms slightly as on all Lateral Raises and maintain that arm bend throughout the movement. Hanging my arms straight down below my shoulder joints, I lightly touch the dumbbells together. Then I slowly raise them in semicircles directly out to the sides and upward until they are at shoulder level. Throughout the

shoulder exercises

movement, my palms are kept facing downward, and at the top of the movement I rotate my thumbs downward as at the top of Standing Dumbbell Side Laterals. Again, this is to strongly stress the medial head of the deltoid muscle. For variety, you can also do this movement on a lower incline, say at 30 degrees. I've even seen some bodybuilders doing the exercise lying facedown on a flat exercise bench, which is equivalent to doing my Seated Bent Laterals.

GENERAL COMMENTS

As mentioned earlier, the front deltoid muscles come strongly into play in most chest exercises. The rear delts are also fairly strongly stressed when you do lat exercises such as Bent Rowing and Chins. Still, you will need to train hard on direct deltoid movements to develop a full and complete deltoid. You must do Overhead Pressing movements for delt mass, Upright Rows for a good delt-trapezius tie-in and various types of Lateral Raises to complete your deltoid development.

In my opinion, most women bodybuilders below the Olympian level tend to have underdeveloped deltoids. So, don't be afraid to really bomb your delts every workout. It's a very difficult muscle to overdevelop.

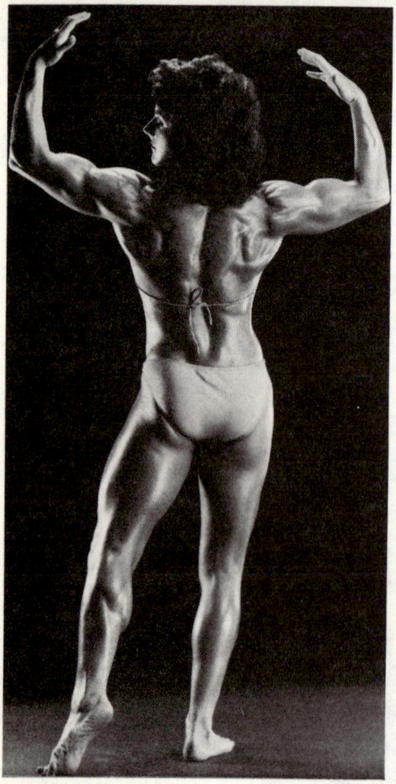

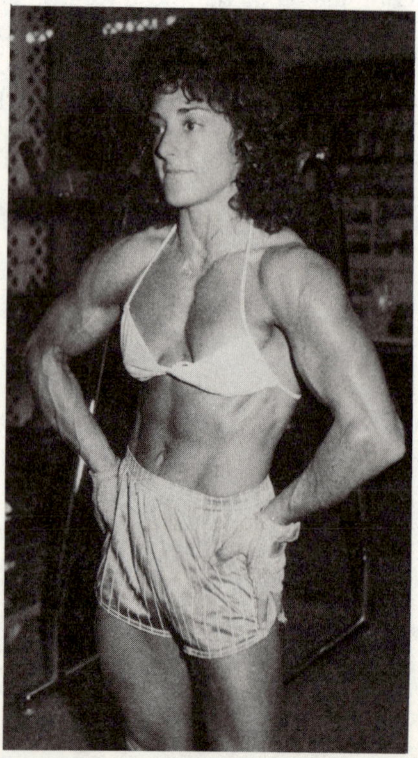

chapter seven
leg and abdominal exercises

The thigh muscles are the largest in the human body and you must expend great quantities of energy to train them hard. As a result, it's rather painful to train thighs and many bodybuilders avoid working their thighs hard enough to really build them up. I used to feel this way myself, but through proper mental programming (see Chapter 10) I have been able to convince myself that heavy leg work is actually enjoyable. And it **is,** because you really know you've put everything you have into a workout when you're covered with sweat and standing on legs that feel like spaghetti at the end of a training session.

The quadriceps muscles on the front of your thigh contract to extend your leg from a bent position. The sartorius—one of the quad muscles—also contracts to pull your legs inward toward each other. The biceps femoris muscles on the back of your thigh have the opposite function to that of your quads—they contract to bend your leg from a straight position.

There are two major muscle groups on the lower leg that you will train hard, and both contract to extend your foot and toes. The gastrocnemius does this while your legs are held straight, but you can only contract your soleus muscles fully when your legs are bent at a 90-degree angle.

You have three major muscle groups making up your abdominal region. The rectus abdominis on the front of your abdomen contracts to bend your body at the waist. Your external obliques contract to bend your torso from side to side, as well as to twist it from side to side. And your intercostal muscles contract to depress your ribs, as well as to help shorten your torso by pulling your shoulders toward your hips.

SQUATS

This is the best of all lower body movements, and many bodybuilders consider it to be the best single exercise available for their use. Certainly, no bodybuilder has ever maximized her thigh development without doing Squats. In addition to stressing the front thigh muscles quite hard, Squats secondarily stress the hamstrings, lower back, abdomen, and upper back muscles.

I bunch up my traps and rest the loaded bar across my shoulders with my traps as a pad. Then I lift the bar from the rack, step back and set my feet with my heels at about shoulder width, my toes pointed slightly outward. I rest my heels on a 2 × 4-inch board for better balance. Then, keeping my torso perfectly upright, I squat down to rock bottom, or until the backs of my thighs contact my calves. Without bouncing at the bottom, I slowly return to the starting position. In the off-season I use heavier weights and squat down only until my thighs are parallel to the floor. For maximum muscle quality close to a competition, however, I feel I need to go to a rock bottom position on each rep as I do my Squats.

Squat.

HACK SQUATS

While it is possible to do this movement with just a barbell, I do it on a machine, as do most bodybuilders I know. Two versions of a hack machine exist, one with a yoke that rests across your shoulders and the other with a sliding platform and two handles to grasp at the bottom edge of the platform. I more often use the latter version. I place my heels in a narrow stance (6–8 inches between my heels) on the angled foot platform, and I point my toes outward at approximately 45-degree angles on each side. Then, as I sink completely into the movement, I make sure my legs angle outward at 45 degrees on each side. Even in the off-season, I go rock-bottom on my Hack Squats.

LEG PRESS

There are horizontal Leg Press machines and machines that allow you to press the weight out at a 45-degree angle, but I prefer to use a vertical Leg Press machine. It's important to lie on the angled pad beneath the machine with your hips set directly under the platform and at the high end of the pad. Any other hip position could put your lower back in a vulnerable position. I place my feet on the movement platform in the same position as for Squats. Then I release the platform stops and do my movement. When you are using extremely heavy weights, be careful to let your knees down on each side of your chest, to avoid breaking a rib. (It *has* happened!) Leg Presses are an excellent mass-building movement for the thighs.

LUNGES

This is an exercise that I use religiously close to a contest, since it is excellent for cutting up the front thighs, particularly up near the hips. Lunges also firm and round the buttocks. While this movement can be done with a pair of dumbbells in your hands, I personally feel better balanced when I do it with a barbell behind my neck as if preparing to Squat. Starting with my feet parallel, I step out as far as I can with my left foot. Then, keeping my right leg as straight as possible, I fully bend my left leg until my knee is several inches ahead of my foot. In this low position, you should feel a strong stretch in the front thigh muscles of your back leg. Finally, I push back to the starting point and repeat the movement with my right foot forward.

LEG EXTENSIONS

This is an excellent movement for cutting up and shaping the front thigh muscles. A Nautilus Leg Extension Machine is best, because it gives you a strong degree of resistance throughout the movement, but any leg extension machine will be good for this

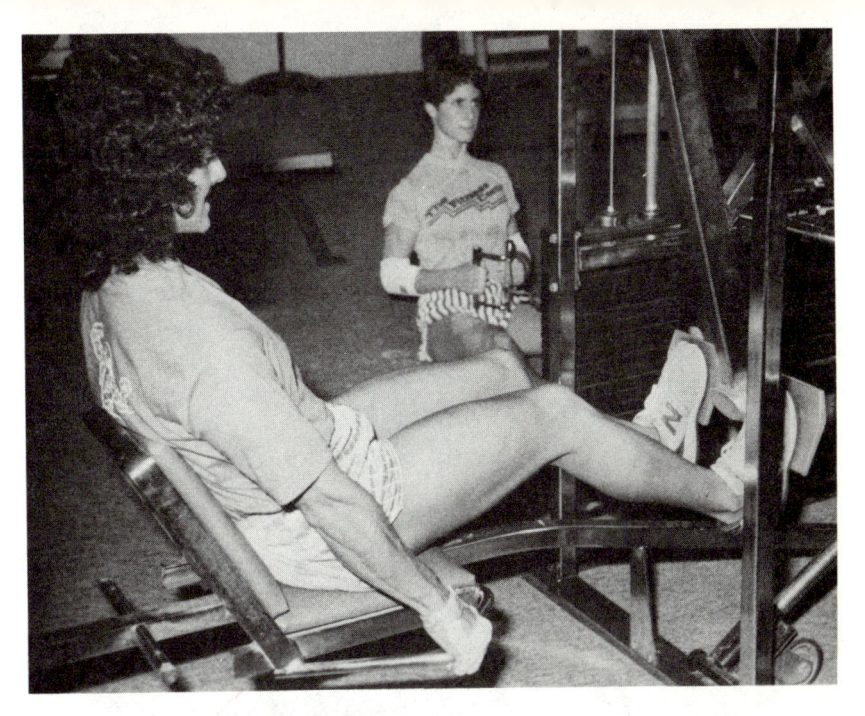

Leg Press, above; Lunge, below.

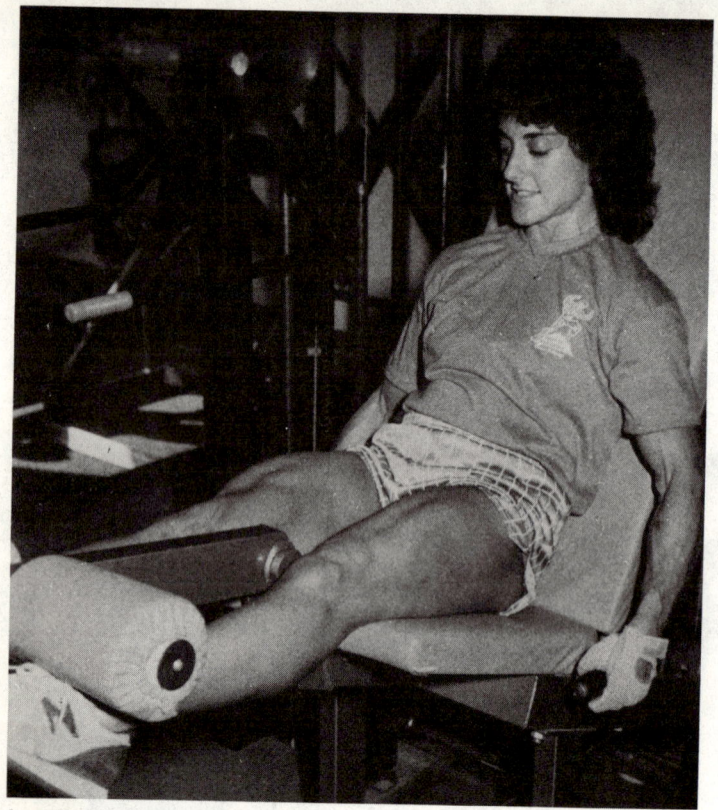

Leg Extension.

movement. I personally don't have access to the Nautilus machine very often, and it hasn't seemed to hold back my thigh development. The key to getting maximum benefit from Leg Extensions is to hold your legs straight at the top of the movement for two or three seconds on each repetition. This gives the muscles a very strong peak contraction effect.

LEG CURLS

I do two types of Leg Curls, one with both legs while lying on my stomach, and another version with one leg at a time while standing. Both variations are quite good, and I do them both because they feel a little different from each other. In the lying variation, it is essential that you keep your hips on the padded surface of the machine throughout the movement, since raising your hips

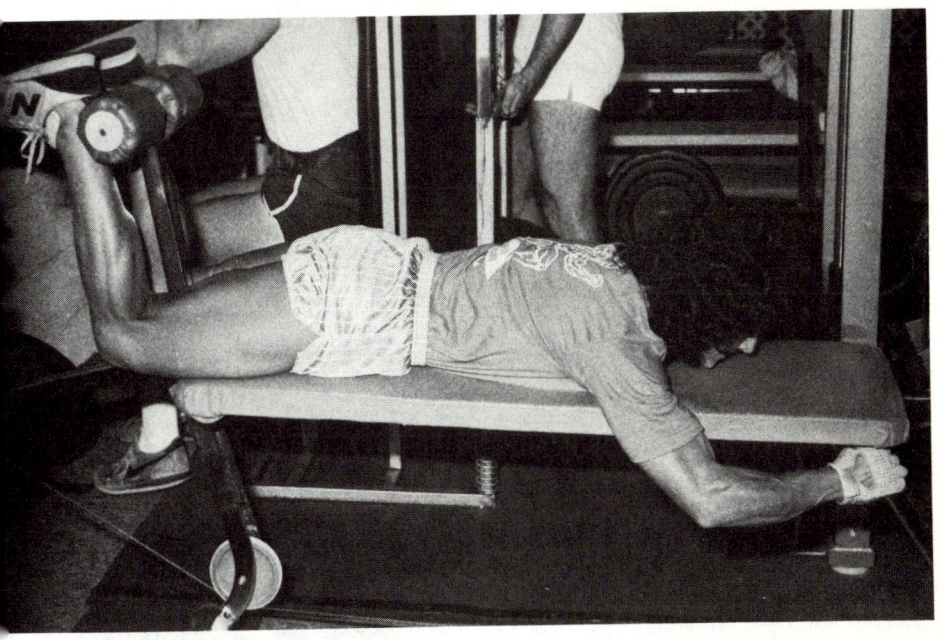

Lying Leg Curl.

shortens the range of motion of the exercise. On both the standing and lying versions of Leg Curls, you should hold the top position of the movement for two or three seconds for a peak contraction effect in your hamstrings (biceps femoris muscles).

ONE-LEG CALF RAISE

I really like this movement, either in high reps with no added weight or in lower repetitions while holding a dumbbell in one hand to add resistance to the exercise. I place the toes and ball of one foot on a block of wood and curl my other leg up out of the way. Then I sag my heel as far below the level of my toes as possible before rising up on my toes as high as I can. If I use a dumbbell I hold it at the side of my leg in the same hand as the leg I am exercising (right leg, right hand, etc.). You will be tempted at times to pull upward with the hand with which you are balancing yourself, but avoid the temptation unless you are specifically trying to give yourself forced reps.

One-Leg Calf Raise.

STANDING CALF MACHINE TOE RAISE

This is the most basic of all calf exercises, and it strongly stresses the gastrocnemius muscles. I place the yoke of the machine across my shoulders and put my toes and the balls of my feet on a high block of wood. Then I do my Toe Raises in that position with the resistance provided by the machine. Some bodybuilders do this movement with their legs slightly bent, while others do it with their legs straight. Try both methods and see which works best for you. It's difficult to use varied toe positions on One-Leg Toe Raises, but for Toe Raises on a standing calf machine and other machines, you should do some sets with your toes pointed directly forward, some with your toes angled outward at 45 degrees on each side, and some with your toes angled inward at 45 degrees on each side. You can also vary the distance between your toes as you do the movement. Most bodybuilders do Toe Raises

leg and abdominal exercises

with their toes at about shoulder width, but you will feel a very different effect on your calves if you move your feet out past this distance or inward closer to each other. On all calf movements, the more variety you can put into them, the more calf development you can expect from your training.

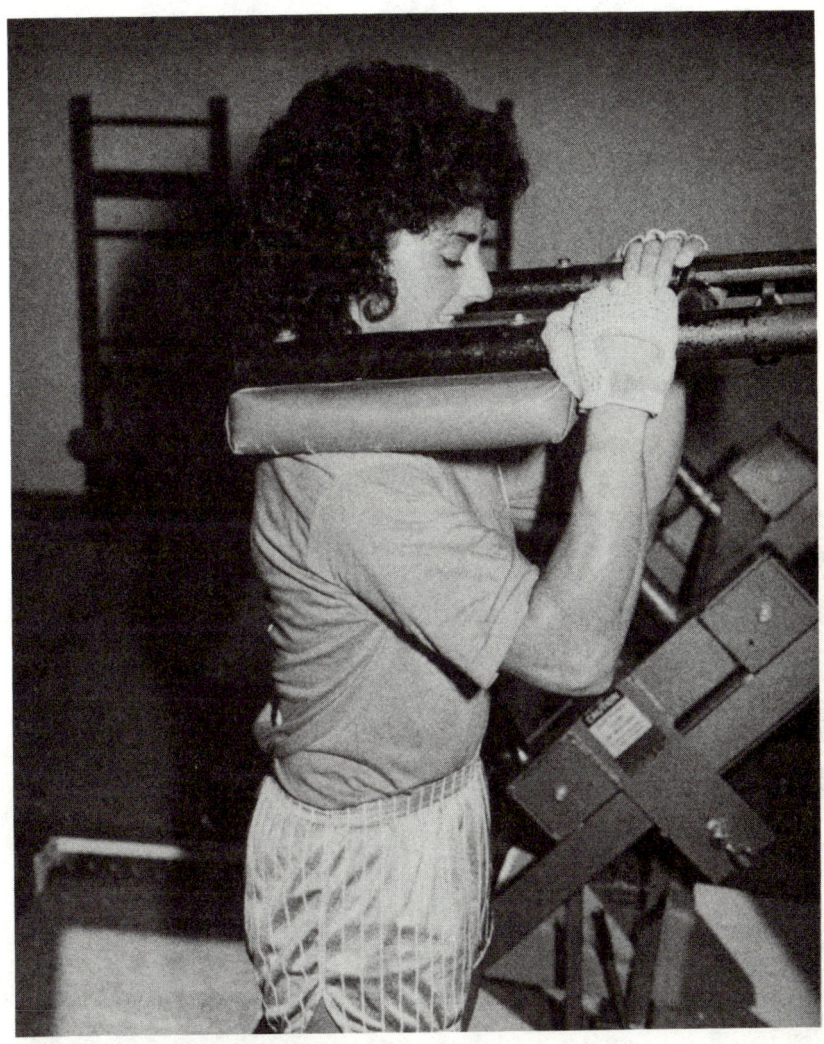

Standing Calf Machine Toe Raise.

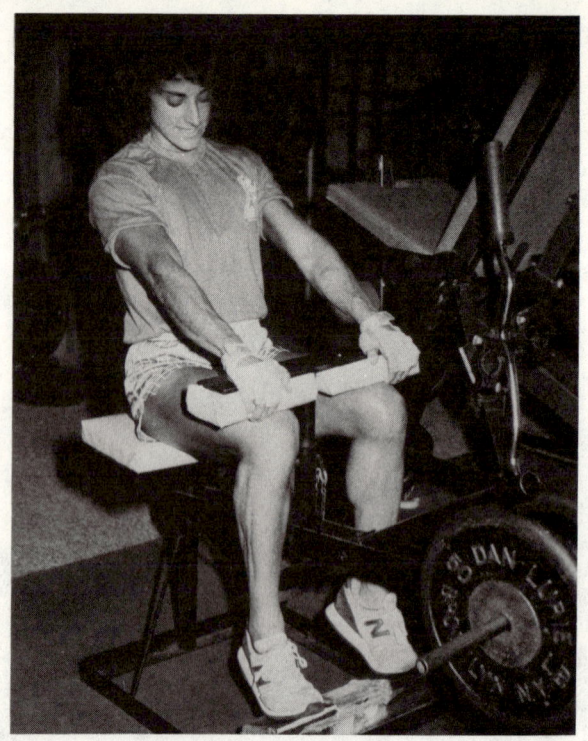

Seated Calf Machine Toe Raise.

Calf Press.

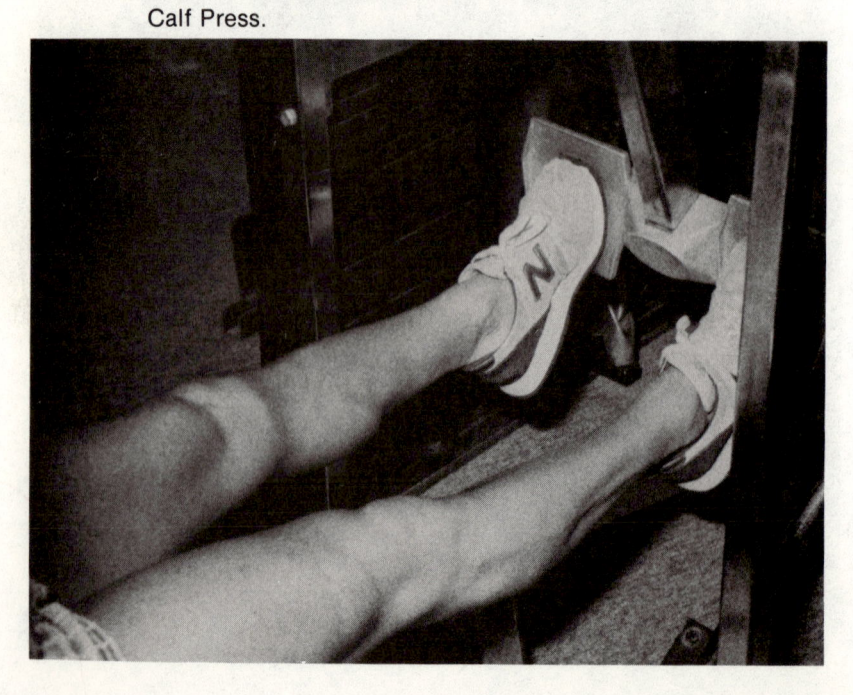

leg and abdominal exercises

SEATED CALF MACHINE TOE RAISE

This movement is relatively new, and it's the best one for developing the broad soleus muscle lying under your gastrocnemius, since it is done with your knees bent at 90 degrees. Prior to the advent of this machine, bodybuilders did this movement by padding a heavy barbell and resting it across their knees, so if you don't have a seated calf machine handy, you can still do the movement in this manner. It's just that the machine is handier to use. Once you place your toes and the balls of your feet on the toe board of the machine and release the stop bar, all you need to do is lower your heels as far as possible and then slowly rise up on your toes as high as possible. Generally speaking, I have found that the soleus muscles tend to respond better to lower reps than do the gastrocnemius muscles. As with Toe Raises on a standing calf machine, you should vary your toe angle occasionally.

CALF PRESS

This fine gastrocnemius exercise is done on a vertical leg press machine. I lie on my back in the machine and press the sliding platform entirely out, e.g. until my legs are straight. Then I carefully move my feet to the edge of the platform so only my toes and the balls of my feet are in contact with the edge of the platform. Then from that position I stretch my calves by allowing my toes to descend as far as possible below the level of my heels before pressing the platform up as high as I can by extending my toes and feet. You can use all three toe angles on this movement.

DONKEY CALF RAISE

I've found this to be one of my favorite movements, but it's one in which I can use about 250 pounds of weight on my hips and back. So, unless I can find a 250-pound male bodybuilder to help me, I need to have two lighter individuals totaling the same weight astride my hips and lower back. Once you have your toes on the

Donkey Calf Raise.

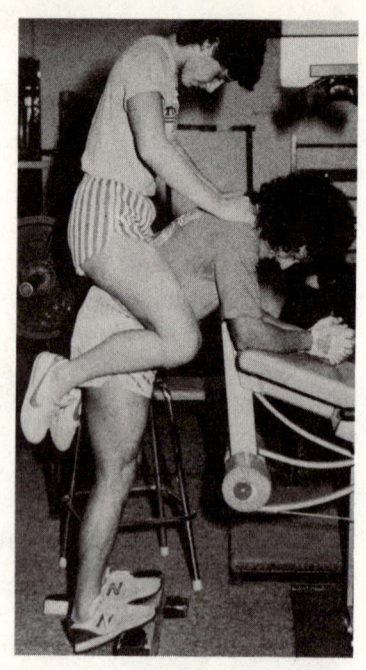

block of wood, you can either rest your hands with your arms straight on a flat exercise bench to balance your body in position, or rest your forearms and head on a higher padded bench. Your heavy partners then jump up astride your hips as though they were cowpokes riding a horse (you). Then, with their added resistance to the movement, sag your heels below your toes and raise up as high as possible on your toes. Be sure to use all three toe angles on this exercise.

INCLINE SIT-UPS

All types of Sit-Ups stress your front abdominal muscles, but particularly the upper half of the rectus abdominis. I raise the foot end of the board up to place the board at a 30- to 45-degree angle (the higher the angle of the bench, the more stress you place on your abdominals as you do the Sit-Ups). I am careful to keep my legs bent at about a 30-degree angle, since this takes potential strain off my lower back muscles. You should *never* do either Sit-Ups or Leg Raises with straight legs, since this puts your lower back in an unfavorable mechanical position. I place my hands

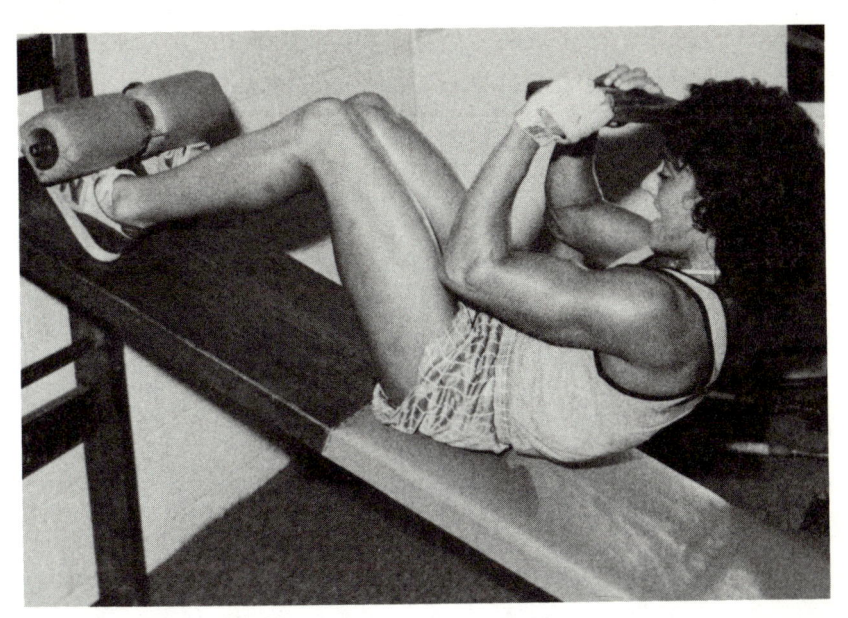

Weighted Incline Sit-Up.

either behind my neck or rest my fists on my forehead and do my Sit-Ups straight forward. I've found that twisting tends to build up my obliques, which in turn makes my waist look unesthetically wider. Toward a contest when I wish additional front abdominal training intensity, I will hold a 10-pound barbell plate on my forehead as I do the movement.

HANGING LEG RAISES

You will find this to be a very intense front abdominal exercise that particularly stresses the lower half of your rectus abdominis. I jump up to hang with my body straight down from a chinning bar. Then I bend my legs slightly to take strain off my lower back, and I keep them bent like this throughout the movement. From the hang position, I raise my feet in a semicircle forward and upward until they are well above the level of my hips. Actually, the higher you raise your knees in this movement the better. If you find that you have difficulty with swinging back and forth under the bar as you do Hanging Leg Raises, have a training partner place his or her hands against the small of your back to retard the swinging.

Hanging Leg Raise.

Bench Leg Raise.

BENCH LEG RAISES

This is a less intense front and lower abdominal movement, so I ordinarily do it somewhere in my abdominal routine after the Hanging Leg Raises. Lie on your back on a flat exercise bench with your hips positioned at the edge of the bench. Grasp the edges of the bench behind your head to steady your body, or place your palms flat on the bench beneath your buttocks as you do the movement. Bend your legs slightly and keep them bent throughout the set. Then lower your feet below the level of the bench and raise them in a semicircle upward until you feel stress lessening on your abdominal muscles. You *can* raise your feet up until they are directly above your hips, but usually you will feel stress beginning to lessen on your abdominals once your thighs are at about a 45-degree angle with the floor. Lower your feet back down and repeat the movement.

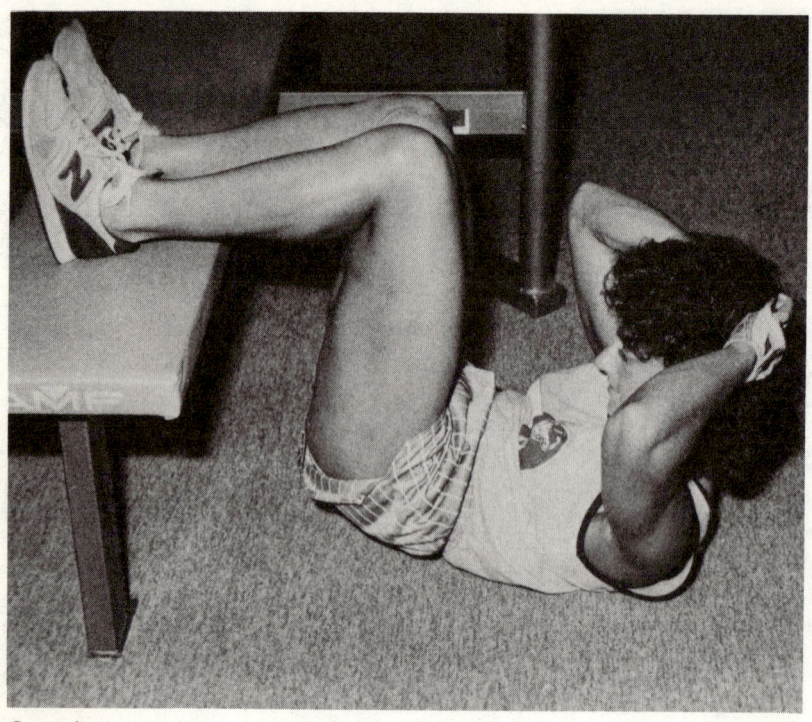

Crunch.

CRUNCHES

I feel this exercise along my entire front abdominal wall, but perhaps a bit more in the upper abs. I lie on my back on the floor with my body perpendicular to a flat exercise bench. Then I drape my lower legs over the bench so my thighs are perpendicular to the floor. You can either interlace your fingers behind your neck or hold your arms across your chest. As you do a Crunch rep, four things must happen simultaneously—your head and shoulders must slowly come off the floor, your hips slowly come off the floor, your shoulders are forced toward your hips, and all of your air is forcefully blown out. When you do these four acts simultaneously, you will feel a very strong contraction in your front abdomen. Hold this contraction for a moment and return to the starting position to repeat the movement.

leg and abdominal exercises

GENERAL COMMENTS

In this chapter, I have discussed exercises for the entire lower half of your body. Train these muscle groups long and hard, and you will have impressive legs and abdominals onstage at a competition. Don't make the common mistake of doing 20 total sets of upper arm work and only 8–10 sets of thigh or calf work. If you're a pumper instead of a chipmunk, you'll *blast* your legs!

Photo by Bill Reynolds.

chapter eight
arm exercises

The two-headed biceps muscles on your upper arm contract to bend your arm fully from a straight position. The biceps also contract to supinate your hand (i.e., to rotate it from a position with your palm down to a position with your palm up). Beneath the biceps lies the flat brachialis muscle, which contracts to bend the arm when your palm is down, as in doing Reverse Curls. The three-headed triceps muscles at the back of your upper arm contract to fully extend the arm from a bent position. The muscles of the forearms contract to either flex or extend your hands and fingers. Most commonly, the muscles of your forearms come into play whenever you are grasping some object.

STANDING BARBELL CURL

This is the most basic of all biceps movements, and it's generally

Standing Barbell Curl.

one of the first weight training exercises most women learn to do. It also has a beneficial effect on your forearm muscles. I use an undergrip on the bar with my hands set slightly wider than the width of my shoulders. Pinning my upper arms against the sides of my lats, I use my biceps strength to move the barbell in a semicircle from the tops of my thighs to my chin. Then I *slowly* lower the barbell back to the starting point. On all but the last few reps of a set, I am careful to avoid swinging my body back and forth to cheat up the weight. I use cheating only to push my biceps past the point where they would normally fail to perform because of fatigue. If you have difficulty doing this movement strictly, I suggest that you perform it while resting your back against a wall.

arm exercises

BARBELL PREACHER CURLS

I do Preacher Curls with my palms up and with my palms down (e.g., with a reversed grip). With my palms up, the movement generally thickens my biceps, but it places greater stress on my lower biceps down near the elbow than on any other part of the muscle group. When I do Preacher Curls with my palms down, it strongly stresses my brachialis muscles and the large supinator muscle on the upper and outer part of my forearm. I use an EZ-Curl bar for both versions of the Preacher Curl, and I also use a shoulder-width grip for both variations. I particularly like this movement, because as long as you are careful to fully straighten your arms at the bottom of the exercise, it is impossible to cheat when doing Preacher Curls.

Barbell Preacher Curl.

STANDING ALTERNATE DUMBBELL CURL

While it is important to supinate your hands as you do Dumbbell Curls, I often do this movement with my thumbs up, which simply tends to hit my biceps from one more new angle. By beginning to curl one dumbbell upward as the other begins to descend (it's sort of a seesaw movement), you can effectively avoid cheating. I would suggest doing about half of your sets with your thumbs up and the other half supinating your hands. When supinating your hands, start the movement with your palms toward your thighs. Then, as you curl the dumbbells upward, simultaneously rotate your palms so they are pointed upward. Two other variations of Dumbbell Curls are done either while seated at the end of a flat exercise bench or while curling both dumbbells at once.

CABLE CURLS

I find this exercise to be excellent for shaping and cutting up my biceps. I do it one arm at a time, with the side of my body with the working arm facing the floor pulley. I grasp the pulley handle, stand erect and then curl the handle slowly and deliberately up to my shoulder. My elbow is away from my body and directly out to the side rather than toward the front as with most types of Curls. Throughout the movement, I keep my palm upward.

CONCENTRATION CURLS

If you have the potential to develop a biceps with a high peak, this movement will bring the peak out. But nothing will give you a Matterhorn peak if you weren't born with the genetic potential for one. I sit at the end of a flat exercise bench with my feet set about 2½ feet apart. I grasp a dumbbell with my right hand and rest my right elbow against the inside of my right thigh about six inches in from my knee. I fully straighten my right arm and rotate my hand so my palm will be facing upward throughout the

Standing Alternate Dumbbell Curl.

Cable Curl.

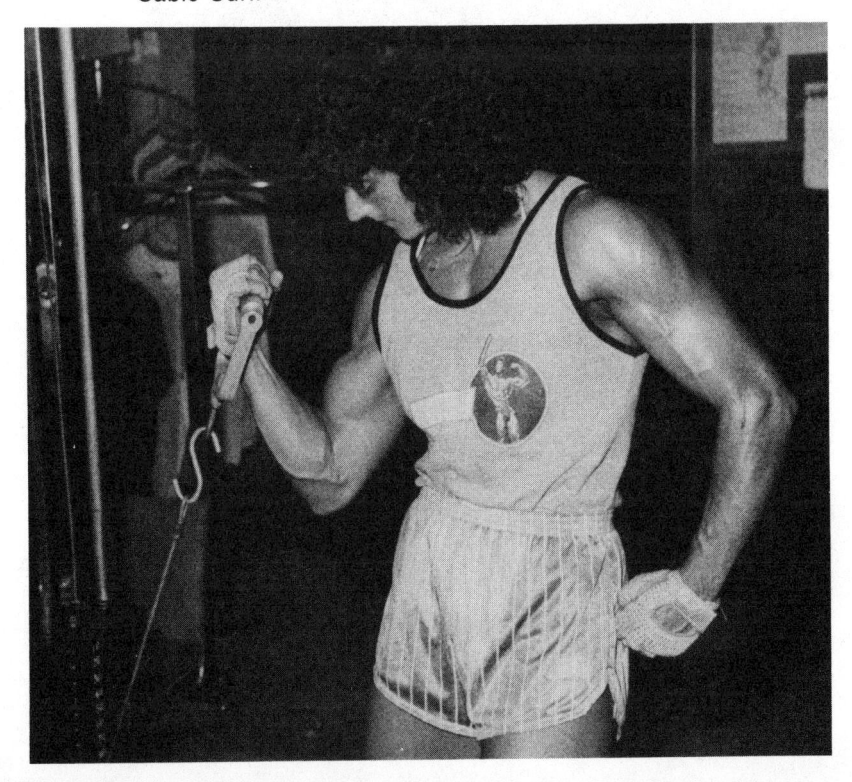

Concentration Curl.

movement. I place my free left hand on my left thigh throughout the movement. From this basic starting position, I slowly curl the dumbbell upward as far as I can, which is almost to the point of touching my right shoulder. I hold the top position for a couple of seconds in order to feel a good peak contraction in my biceps before lowering the dumbbell back to the starting position. As with all one-armed exercises, I am careful to do an equal number of sets and reps with each arm. As a general exercise tip, if you have one arm that is consistently weaker than the other, you should always do your set for that arm first, so you won't continue to do more for your already stronger arm.

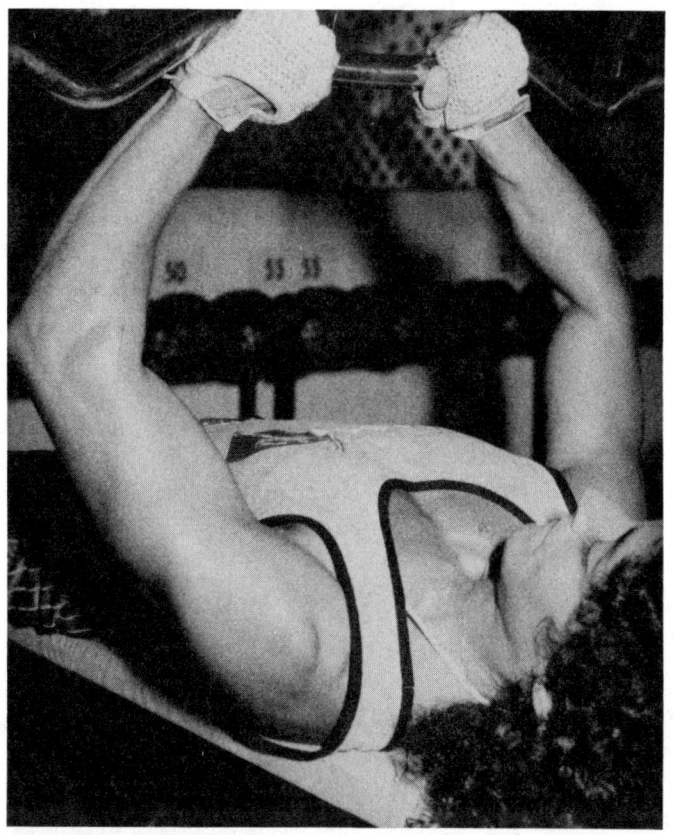

Close-Grip Bench Press.

CLOSE-GRIP BENCH PRESS

This is my most basic triceps exercise, and it's the best I have found for bulking the muscle. As an added bonus, you will find that Close-Grip Bench Presses add mass to your inner pecs. I use an EZ-Curl bar for this exercise and take a narrow grip on the bar (about six inches between my index fingers). Starting with my arms straight and the bar directly above my shoulder joints, I slowly lower it downward to touch my upper chest, allowing my upper arms to travel a little forward of a position directly out to the sides of my torso. Then I slowly push the bar back to arms' length and strongly flex my triceps in this position before starting another repetition.

LYING BARBELL TRICEPS EXTENSION

This movement is similar to the Close-Grip Bench Presses because it is good for adding to triceps mass and you start in exactly the same position with an EZ-Curl bar (you will have to use a lighter weight, however). From the starting position, be sure that you don't allow your upper arms to move while you are doing the exercise. Simply bend your elbows and slowly lower the barbell in a semicircle from the starting position until it touches your forehead. Then, using only the strength of your triceps, return the barbell along the same arc as you lower it back to the starting point. Lying Barbell Triceps Extensions are a particularly good movement for bulking the large inner head of your triceps.

STANDING ONE-ARM DUMBBELL TRICEPS EXTENSION

I've done Dumbbell Triceps Extensions with both arms simultaneously, but have found that I can concentrate harder on the movement when I am doing it one arm at a time. And when I can concentrate harder, I invariably get more out of an exercise. Standing erect with a light dumbbell in my right hand, I extend my arm directly up from my shoulder joint and restrain my upper arm in this position throughout the movement. Then I slowly bend my elbow and lower the dumbbell downward in a semicircle behind my neck until my arm is fully bent. Finally, using only triceps strength, I return it along the same arc to the starting point.

PULLEY PUSHDOWNS

Many bodybuilders favor a short angled handle for this movement, but I prefer to do it with the same long straight bar that I use for my Lat Pulldowns. For some reason I simply feel more in my triceps when I use this bar. The key to effectively using pushdowns is to keep your upper arms pressed against your lats,

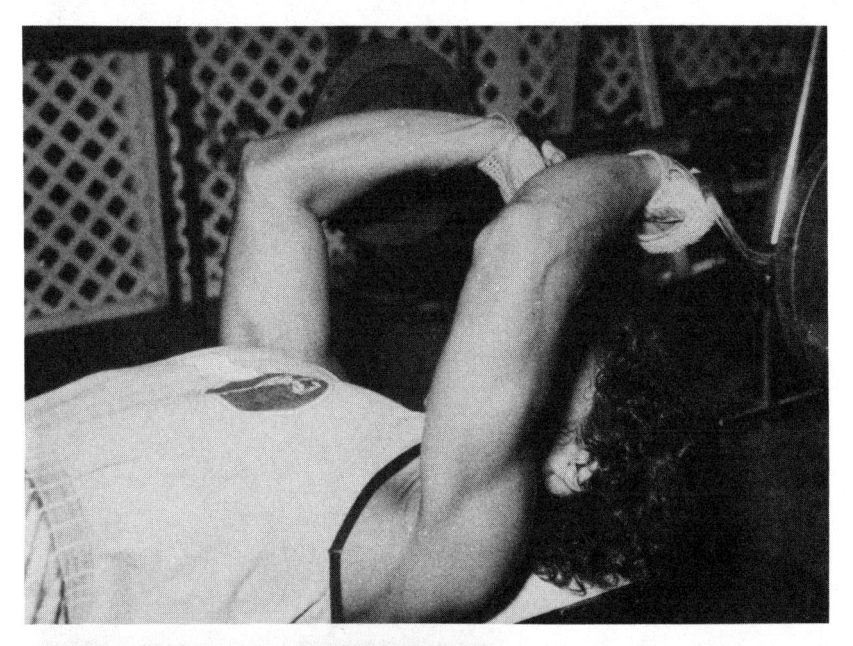

Lying Barbell Triceps Extension, above; Standing One-Arm Dumbbell Triceps Extension, left.

Pulley Pushdown.

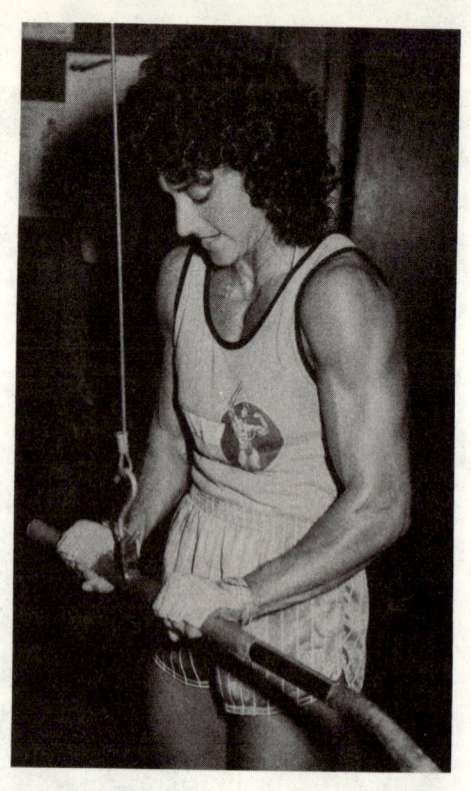

begin with the bar up under your chin and slowly press it down until your arms are perfectly straight. I also hold this finish position for a couple of counts to get a good peak contraction effect in my triceps. You will find that Pushdowns are an excellent movement for stressing the outer head of your triceps quite hard.

ONE-ARM TRICEPS KICKBACKS

I do this movement quite a bit differently than most bodybuilders, but my method seems to allow me to get a very good peak contraction effect in my triceps while using a heavier weight than most bodybuilders can handle doing their version of the exercise. I take a heavy dumbbell in my right hand while standing erect. Then I bend forward at the waist just enough so I can rest my left hand on my left thigh to brace my body in position during the movement. Next I bend my right arm and brace my right upper arm in a position where it is slightly above an imaginary

One-Arm Triceps Kickback.

line drawn at a 45-degree angle with the floor. I maintain this upper arm position throughout the movement. With this starting position established, I simply straighten my right arm as forcefully as possible. It's a rather short movement, but I can feel it quite strongly throughout my triceps muscle. Again, I am careful to do an equal number of sets and repetitions for both arms.

BARBELL WRIST CURL

This exercise can be done with the palms up to strongly stress the muscles on the insides of your forearms, or with your palms down to stress the muscles on the outsides of your forearms. You will actually have to do both variations of the movement if you wish to achieve optimum forearm development. I sit astride a flat exercise bench with a grip on the bar that has my palms up and my little fingers only about four or five inches apart. Then I run my forearms down the bench so my wrists and fists are hanging off the edge of the bench. From this position, I extend my hands and allow the bar to actually roll out of my hands and down to the tips of my fingers. Finally, I flex my fingers to roll the bar

Barbell Wrist Curl—palms up, left; palms down, right.

back up into my hands and fully flex my wrists, curling the barbell in a little semicircle up as high as I can before lowering it back down. When I do the movement palms down, it is a reverse curling movement only—you can't roll the bar down to your fingertips. Generally speaking, you will find that you can use approximately twice as much weight with your palms upward as you can when you have your palms facing downward.

STANDING WRIST CURL

This is a good movement for stressing the inner parts of your forearms with peak contraction. It can be done with either two dumbbells or a barbell. In the dumbbell version, you should stand erect with two dumbbells hanging down at your sides. Your arms should be straight and your palms should be toward your legs. From this position, simultaneously curl the dumbbells upward in small semicircles as high as you can by flexing your wrists. Hold this top position for a second or two for the peak contraction effect before lowering the dumbbells back down to the starting point.

When using a barbell, you should hold it behind your thighs

Standing Barbell Wrist Curl, left; Standing Dumbbell Wrist Curl, right.

and buttocks with your palms facing the rear. Your arms should be straight and you should have a grip on the bar slightly wider than the width of your shoulders. You will find it easiest to get a heavy barbell into this position if you first rest it on a bench press rack and load it up before backing up to the rack and grasping the barbell. Once you have it in position behind your legs, however, curl it up to the rear in a small semicircle as high as you can by fully flexing your wrists. Again, hold the top position as long as you can to achieve a peak contraction effect in your forearm muscles.

GENERAL COMMENTS

Virtually all bodybuilders—whether women or men—enjoy doing upper arm work, but many neglect training their forearms hard enough. They receive a minimum of forearm development from gripping barbells, dumbbells, and various other exercise apparatus, but it takes consistent direct forearm training to fully develop the lower arms. A winning bodybuilder is usually one with no underpar body parts, so never neglect working on your forearm development!

Photo by Mike Neveux.

chapter nine
bodybuilding routines

Now that you are thoroughly familiar with the exercises I use in my training, I will discuss several advanced-level bodybuilding techniques and then outline three advanced training routines using the exercises in chapters 4-8. You can begin using the first of these routines immediately if you have at least three or four months of steady weight training behind you.

The topics I will discuss in this chapter include the relationship between strength and muscle mass; overtraining and training layoffs; sources of inspiration; bodybuilding training instinct; split routines; and how to formulate your own workout programs.

STRENGTH AND MUSCLE MASS

Throughout your bodybuilding career, there will be a lifetime marriage between the strength and mass of your muscles. There is a direct relationship between the amount of weight you can handle in strict form for several reps in an exercise and the ultimate mass of the muscles that move the weight in that exercise. The more weight you lift, the larger your muscles will be.

As pointed out in Chapter 2 in the discussion of how training works, a steady progression of resistance is at the heart of success in bodybuilding training. You use a slightly heavier weight on an exercise than your muscles are used to handling, so they grow in mass and strength to handle this heavier weight. And as soon as they have grown larger and stronger to accommodate the heavier weight, you bomb them with an even heavier poundage. In this way, you literally force your muscles to slowly and steadily increase in mass and strength.

Keep in mind, however, that using loose exercise form merely to handle a little heavier weight in an exercise does very little to encourage muscle hypertrophy. Neither does lifting a very heavy weight for only one or two repetitions. That only makes you strong at doing singles or doubles in an exercise. What most quickly stimulates muscle hypertrophy is the use of progressively heavier and heavier weights in strict exercise form for at least four or five repetitions per set.

In Chapter 11, I describe in detail exactly how I cycle my training over the course of a year to improve my physique from one year to the next. Like all bodybuilders I have a long off-season muscle-building cycle followed by a shorter, sharpening-and-defining, precontest cycle.

Emphasis during an off-season cycle—which can last from 3-9 months for a competitive bodybuilder—should be placed equally on substantially improving lagging body parts and generally adding muscle mass to the body. When I'm dieting strictly and training specifically for cuts during a precontest cycle, it's virtually impossible to increase my muscle mass. It's only during the off-season when I can consume enough calories to train heavy for increased power that I add substantially to my overall muscle mass.

bodybuilding routines

If you haven't yet competed as a bodybuilder, you are still on a long muscle-building off-season cycle. But if you are already in competition, don't make the common mistake of constantly dieting and training on a precontest routine so you can compete every couple of weeks for an extended period of time. You may collect a few titles and a lot of trophies that way, but you will not be able to add much muscle mass to your body.

I compete only once a year in the Miss Olympia contest, the most prestigious professional event for women bodybuilders to enter. Therefore, I have an off-season building cycle that lasts approximately nine months, followed by a three-month precontest cycle.

If you are already competing, I am convinced that you'll make better overall progress as a bodybuilder if you compete only twice a year, preferably at six-month intervals. This will allow you to train for power and mass during a four-month off-season cycle, enough time to add appreciable muscle tissue to your body. Then you can spend two months sharpening and defining the muscles you've built in the off-season. You'll win fewer trophies this way, but ultimately, you'll win titles at a much higher level than if you try to compete every weekend.

Pyramid Power

The best way to build power—and hence mass—in the off-season is to pyramid your reps and poundages on succeeding sets of an exercise. Pyramidding involves increasing the weight you use on a movement while decreasing the number of reps you perform on each succeeding set. And the advantage of pyramidding is that it allows you to warm up thoroughly before using your heaviest training poundages.

Pyramidding is the quickest way to build the power which will increase your muscle mass. I've seen numerous, fairly experienced women bodybuilders increase their Squat training weights by 5-10 pounds per week for an extended period of time by pyramidding their weights and reps.

To avoid confusion, let me illustrate a pyramid in action. Let's assume that you are doing five sets of Squats in your off-season leg workout. In such a case, your pyramid might look like this:

Set Number	Exercise Weight	Reps
1	100	12
2	125	10
3	140	8
4	150	6
5	160	4–5

The weights listed are irrelevant for most of you—since individual strength levels vary so widely—but I'm sure you will get the idea of how pyramidding works. You should also understand that pyramidding will do nothing for you during a precontest phase, but in the off-season it will allow you very quickly to increase both your strength and muscle mass.

BASIC vs. ISOLATION MOVEMENTS

Tying in with the concept of off-season and precontest cycles is the concept of basic versus isolation exercises. Basic movements work large body parts in combination with smaller muscle groups, and you can use very heavy weights on them. Isolation exercises, on the other hand, work single muscles—or even segments of a muscle group—in relative isolation from the rest of the body. And, you can't use much weight on most isolation exercises.

Because you can use heavy weights to stress the large muscle groups of your body with basic exercises, they are quite appropriate for use in building power and muscle mass during the off-season. During my off-season cycle, I tend to use predominantly basic exercises; I push some heavy iron on them.

In contrast, isolation movements are most appropriate for use prior to a competition, because they are very good for shaping

bodybuilding routines

and detailing each muscle group. Prior to a contest I use plenty of isolation exercises, including several using cables for resistance (when I have the cables available). Still, I will always do at least one or two basic exercises per muscle group prior to competing in order to maintain as much muscle mass and fullness in my muscles as possible while I am defining them.

So you will not be confused about what is a basic movement and an isolation exercise, here are lists of both types of exercises for each major muscle group:

	Basic Exercise	*Isolation Exercise*
Chest	Bench Press Incline Barbell Press	Incline Flyes Cable Crossovers
Back	Barbell Bent Rowing T-Bar Rowing Seated Pulley Rowing	One-Arm Cable Rowing Close-Grip Lat Pulldowns Pullovers
Shoulders	Military Press Dumbbell Press Upright Rowing	Side Laterals Seated Bent Laterals Front Raises
Thighs	Squats Leg Presses	Leg Extensions Leg Curls
Arms	Standing Barbell Curl Preacher Curls Close-Grip Bench Press Lying Triceps Extension	Concentration Curls Cable Curls Pulley Pushdown Triceps Kickbacks

The salient point in discussing basic and isolation exercises, again, is that basic exercises with heavy weights develop mass and power, while isolation movements with lighter weights build muscle shape and detail.

OVERTRAINING AND LAYOFFS

Virtually every competitive bodybuilder overtrains one or more times during her career. Indeed, there is such a fine line between training with optimum intensity and overtraining that it's relatively easy to stumble over that line. Also, to reach peak competitive condition you often have to overtrain a bit.

Overtraining can be defined as doing so much training that your body and mind fail to fully recuperate between workouts. Like your checking account in which you write checks and make deposits, you consume energy in training and replenish it while resting and sleeping. And, as with overdrawing on your checking account, you can go "energy broke" if you expend energy faster than you can replenish it.

When you are energy broke, you are overtrained. You are literally so physically and/or mentally exhausted that your body breaks down. You end up unable even to face the prospect of going to the gym to train. Indeed, you would probably choose a wrestling match with King Kong over a stiff arm workout when you're overtrained. And when you are badly overtrained, you are very susceptible to injury and illness.

In addition to apathy toward your training, there are several other symptoms of overtraining that you should be aware of:

- elevated morning pulse rate;
- nervousness, irritability, and insomnia;
- persistently sore muscles and/or joints; and
- lack of concentration

The best single solution to overtraining is a short layoff from bodybuilding workouts. Stay out of the gym and wait until you're hungry for a workout again. This happens very quickly, because the longest I've been able to go before beginning to crave a good muscle pump again after overtraining has been only a week.

Once you get back into the gym again, keep firmly in your mind that overtraining results not from training *too hard,* but from training *too much.* Therefore, I recommend that you change

bodybuilding routines

your training program and resolve to do shorter, more intense workouts. In the off-season you'll actually build more muscle mass with short, intense workouts than with lighter, marathon sessions. Save the marathon training for the final few weeks before a competition.

INSPIRATION

One magic ingredient in bodybuilding is inspiration, which keeps up your enthusiasm for training. I receive my greatest inspiration by lying on my back and visualizing the image of how I intend to appear ultimately as a bodybuilder. Then I compare that image with what I actually see in the mirror. The difference between image and reality inspires me—or actually inflames me with desire—to train like a maniac so I will more quickly achieve my ultimate physique.

There are several other ways in which you can gain inspiration and further your bodybuilding progress. Some of these are attending a bodybuilding competition, talking with a champion bodybuilder or attending one of her training seminars, reading bodybuilding books and magazines, and looking through your training diary to see how much you have improved.

I strongly urge you to save all of the bodybuilding magazines you purchase. They are excellent reference sources. But over and above that, they are a great source of inspiration. Whenever I'm a little down and not looking forward to a workout, a half hour of thumbing through my old mags really psychs me up to train. Looking at photos of all the male and female champs in the magazines is a tremendous source of inspiration.

TRAINING INSTINCT

Bodybuilding is like a long and very complex scientific experiment, and your body is your laboratory. Over a period of several years you must experiment with every possible variable of training and nutrition in an effort to discover precisely what works

Checking cuts in the mirror.

best in bringing your own uniquely individual body to peak bodybuilding condition. While you may eventually discover precisely what combination of training and dietary factors it takes to get you into optimum shape in the shortest possible time, it is much more likely that you will continue searching and experimenting for a lifetime. I know that I am still trying new things all the time, and so are all of the other top women bodybuilders I know. Every time we meet, we seem to end up discussing new training and dietary shortcuts that we've discovered.

Experimenting itself isn't enough, however. You also need to develop a way to evaluate the relative success or failure of each experiment. This evaluative tool is your "training instinct." At first you won't have such an instinct, but through constant monitoring of your body's biofeedback signals—that is, by constantly staying in touch with what your body is telling you—this

bodybuilding routines

instinct will gradually emerge. After a couple of years you will be able to tell instinctively, within a matter of hours or days, whether a new training or nutritional technique is working for you simply by the way your body *feels*.

There are a large number of biofeedback signals that your body gives you. Below are some examples:

1. What does hunger mean? (Your body requires food.)
2. Muscle soreness? (Yesterday's workout was harder than what your muscles are accustomed to handling.)
3. Chronic fatigue? (You are sleeping too little, training too much, or both.)
4. A good muscle pump? (The workout you just did for that muscle group was essentially perfect for that point in time.)
5. Body fat accumulating on your hips and thighs? (You are consuming more calories each day than your body needs to meet its metabolic and training requirements.)
6. Easily completing 10 reps in an exercise with a weight that caused you difficulty in completing eight reps a week before? (The muscles that move the weight in that exercise have grown stronger—and a bit larger—very quickly.)

These are only a few examples of the biofeedback signals that you should be alert to as you experiment. By consistently observing them, you'll soon be able to decide instinctively whether a new pectoral routine will give you quicker results in upper pec growth than the one you have been using. And once you have gained such instinctive training ability, you possess one of the most valuable tools that a bodybuilder can have in her training arsenal!

SPLIT ROUTINES

As you have no doubt already discovered, the further you get into bodybuilding, the longer and more involved your training routines become. Early on, you will be doing too much training to be able to accomplish a full-body workout in a single day. You simply won't have enough available energy to do justice to every muscle group under such circumstances.

The solution to this dilemma is to switch to a split routine in which you divide your body into halves or thirds and do only a portion of your entire workout each training day. This involves working out more frequently than three times per week, but it allows you to do shorter training sessions that are well within the capabilities of your energy reserves and which can be of much higher intensity as a result. And, even though you may be training every day, each muscle group can fully recuperate and grow while it rests as another body part is trained.

In the simplest type of split routine, you divide your body into halves and train each half twice a week on a four-day split. Such a split routine allows plenty of time for recuperation and muscle growth, so many lower-level competitive bodybuilders use a four-day split in the off-season when attempting to gain muscle mass. Being much more advanced, however, I train six days per week year-round.

There are several good ways to divide your body into halves for a four-day split. Here are three such alternatives:

Alternative A

Monday-Thursday
Chest
Back
Shoulders
Abdominals

Tuesday-Friday
Thighs
Upper Arms-Forearms
Calves
Abdominals

Alternative B

Monday-Thursday
Thighs
Chest
Biceps
Forearms
Abdominals

Tuesday-Friday
Back
Shoulders
Triceps
Calves
Abdominals

bodybuilding routines

Alternative C

Monday-Thursday	Tuesday-Friday
Chest	Thighs
Shoulders	Back
Triceps	Biceps
Forearms	Calves
Abdominals	Abdominals

Note that on all alternatives the abdominals are trained four times a week. Abs seem to require constant training to keep sleek and strong.

Another good off-season split routine—especially if you are a woman who likes her weekends free for recreational and social pursuits—is a five-day split. When you use a five-day split you will still divide your body into halves using one of the foregoing methods, or one of your own invention. For the sake of illustration, regardless of which alternative you choose, let's call the Monday-Thursday half **X** and the Tuesday-Friday half **Y**.

In a five-day split you will do **X** on Monday, Wednesday, and Friday the first week and **Y** on Tuesday and Thursday. Then during the second week switch to doing **Y** on Monday, Wednesday, and Friday, with **X** on Tuesday and Thursday. Here's a schematic of how this works:

	M	T	W	T	F
Week 1	X	Y	X	Y	X
Week 2	Y	X	Y	X	Y
Week 3	X	Y	X	Y	X

Overall, a five-day split routine has a higher intensity rating than a four-day split. And, I know numerous good women bodybuilders who follow a five-day split in the off-season.

Another step up the intensity ladder is the six-day split routine. There are two types of six-day splits, one in which you work each major muscle group twice a week and another in which each major group is trained three times a week. The second of these two alternatives adds more intensity to your training than the first.

Through long experimentation and the use of my training instinct, I have determined that I make my best gains in overall muscle mass when I hit each major body part twice per week, and I also retain a greater degree of mass during my precontest phase if I stick to the same scheme, even when doing more than one workout per day. No doubt my body needs the extra recuperation time that the twice-a-week scheme allows in order to grow.

Numerous other champion women bodybuilders—among them Carla Dunlap, Pillow, and Lisa Elliott—like a six-day split hitting each major muscle group three times per week during their precontest phase. For these bodybuilders and many others, such a six-day split routine helps to bring out the ultimate degree of muscle hardness, but I would lose mass on it. So, your best bet is to give each type of six-day split routine a good trial and then use your training instinct to determine which is best for you.

In the first type of six-day split routine you have to divide your body into thirds. Here are two alternative methods of doing so:

Alternative A

Mon–Thurs	Tues–Fri	Wed–Sat
Abdominals	Abdominals	Abdominals
Chest	Shoulders	Thighs
Upper Back	Upper Arms	Lower Back
Calves	Forearms	Calves

Alternative B

Mon–Thurs	Tues–Fri	Wed–Sat
Abdominals	Abdominals	Abdominals
Chest	Upper Back	Thighs
Shoulders	Biceps	Lower Back
Triceps	Forearms	Forearms
Calves	Calves	

bodybuilding routines

Notice how I've put abdominal work first in all of these routines. Ab training is an excellent warmup prior to your major session, and it always seems to put me in the correct frame of mind to work out hard. Also, I've tried doing ab work last in my routine and found it to be excessively boring at that point in my workout, so boring in fact that I began to let it slide. At the Olympian level you can't afford to let a workout for any body part slide.

A six-day split routine with each major body part worked three times per week is very easy to figure out, in that it involves dividing your body into halves as in the four-day split and five-day split examples. Then you simply do **X** on Mondays, Wednesdays, and Fridays, with **Y** done on Tuesdays, Thursdays, and Saturdays. And, thank God for Sunday's day of rest, because you'll need it!

THREE ADVANCED ROUTINES

As you learn what exercises and routines work best for your own unique physique, you should take responsibility for making up your own training programs (please see the next section of this chapter for instructions on how to formulate your own routines). I will, however, give you three progressively more difficult advanced bodybuilding routines that you can pump away on in the meantime.

I'd suggest using each of these training programs for six weeks before moving on to the next one. Also, you should keep it firmly in mind that these are *advanced* workouts unsuitable for use by beginners. You will need a minimum of three or four months of hard and steady weight training behind you before you can safely use the Level 1 workout. And, you would actually be better off if you have at least six full months of regular training under your belt before attacking the Level 1 program.

Obviously, I won't need to tell you what exercise weights to use on each movement, since you will have more than adequate experience to determine that for yourself. The exercises in this and the following two training programs are all described and illustrated in Chapters 4–8.

Take note in Level 2 of how the Monday–Thursday and Tuesday–Friday workouts are quite heavy ones for the body's major muscle groups, somewhat as in Level 1. But on Wednesdays and Saturdays at Level 2 you will do full workouts only for abs, calves and forearms. These lighter Wednesday–Saturday sessions will accustom you to training six days per week, as you must in the following workout.

This Level 3 training program is a very tough one to complete each day, but if you happen to be able to just blast through it with unbridled joy, you can bet the house and car that you're a *bodybuilder!*

Level 1 Workout

Monday–Thursday

Exercise	Sets	Reps
1. Incline Sit-Ups	3–4	20
2. Bench Leg Raises	3–4	20
3. Barbell Incline Press	4–5	6–8
4. Pec Deck Flyes	4	8–10
5. Military Press	3	6–8
6. Seated Bent Laterals	3	8–10
7. Upright Rowing	3	8–10
8. Barbell Bent Rowing	4	8–10
9. Wide-Grip Lat Pulldowns	3	8–10
10. Narrow-Grip Lat Pulldowns	3	8–10
11. Standing Calf Machine	5	10–12

bodybuilding routines

Tuesday-Friday

Exercise	Sets	Reps
1. Hanging Leg Raises	3–4	10
2. Crunches	3–4	20
3. Squats	5	8–12
4. Leg Extensions	3	8–12
5. Leg Curls	4	8–12
6. Standing Barbell Curl	3–4	8–10
7. Concentration Curl	3	8–10
8. Close-Grip Bench Press	4	8–10
9. Pulley Pushdowns	3	8–10
10. Standing Barbell Wrist Curl	3–4	10–15
11. Seated Reverse Wrist Curl	3–4	10–15
12. Seated Calf Machine	5	8–10

Level 2 Workout

Monday-Thursday

Exercise	Sets	Reps
1. Hanging Leg Raise	3–4	10–12
2. Bench Press	5	6–8
3. Incline Flyes	4	8–10
4. Cross-Bench Pullovers	3	10–15
5. Dumbbell Press	4	6–8
6. Prone Incline Laterals	3	8–10
7. Seated Bent Laterals	3	8–10
8. Upright Rowing	3	8–10
9. Wide-Grip Chins	4	6–8
10. T-Bar Rowing	4	8–10
11. Seated Pulley Rowing	3–4	8–10
12. Donkey Calf Raise	4–5	10–15

Tuesday–Friday

Exercise	Sets	Reps
1. Incline Sit-Ups	3–4	20–25
2. Squats	4	8–12
3. Leg Presses	4	10–15
4. Leg Extensions	3	8–12
5. Leg Curls	5	8–12
6. Standing Barbell Curl	3	8–10
7. Alternate Dumbbell Curl	2–3	8–10
8. Reverse-Grip Preacher Curl	2–3	8–10
9. Close-Grip Bench Press	4	8–10
10. Lying Triceps Extension	3–4	8–10
11. Triceps Kickbacks	2–3	8–10
12. Barbell Wrist Curls	3–4	10–15

Wednesday–Saturday

Exercise	Sets	Reps
1. Hanging Leg Raises	3	10–15
2. Incline Sit-Ups	3	20–30
3. Bench Leg Raises	3	20–30
4. Crunches	3	20–30
5. One-Leg Calf Raise	4	10–15
6. Seated Calf Machine	3	8–10
7. Calf Press	3	15–20
8. Seated Barbell Wrist Curl	3–4	10–15
9. Seated Reverse Wrist Curl	3–4	10–15
10. Standing Barbell Wrist Curl	3–4	10–15

bodybuilding routines

Level 3 Workout
Monday–Thursday

Exercise	Sets	Reps
1. Hanging Leg Raises	3	10–15
2. Incline Sit-Ups	3	20–30
3. Crunches	3	20–30
4. Bench Press	4	6–8
5. Incline Barbell Press	4	6–8
6. Incline Flyes	3	8–10
7. Pec Deck Flyes	3	8–10
8. Barbell Bent Rowing	4	8–10
9. Wide-Grip Chins	4	6–8
10. Narrow-Grip Lat Pulldown	3–4	8–10
11. One-Arm Cable Rowing	3	8–10
12. Standing Calf Machine	5–8	10–15

Tuesday–Friday

Exercise	Sets	Reps
1. Incline Sit-Ups	3	20–30
2. Bench Leg Raises	3	20–30
3. Crunches	3	20–30
4. Dumbbell Press	1–2	10–15
5. Military Press	4	6–8
6. Side Laterals	3	8–10
7. Seated Bent Laterals	3	8–10
8. Prone Incline Laterals	2–3	8–10
9. Upright Rowing	3	8–10
10. Barbell Preacher Curls	4	8–10
11. Reverse-Grip Preacher Curls	3	8–10
12. Alternate Dumbbell Curls	3	8–10
13. Close-Grip Bench Press	4	8–10
14. One-Arm Dumbbell Extensions	4	8–10
15. Pulley Pushdowns	3–4	8–10
16. Standing Barbell Wrist Curl	4–5	10–15
17. Seated Reverse Wrist Curl	4–5	10–15

Wednesday–Saturday

Exercise	Sets	Reps
1. Hanging Leg Raises	3	10–15
2. Incline Sit-Ups	3	20–30
3. Bench Leg Raises	3	20–30
4. Crunches	3	20–30
5. Squats	5	8–12
6. Hack Squats	4	8–12
7. Leg Extensions	4	8–12
8. Lying Leg Curls	3	8–12
9. Standing Leg Curls	3	8–12
10. Lunges	2–3	10–15
11. Seated Calf Machine	5	8–10
12. Calf Press	5	12–15

ORGANIZING YOUR OWN WORKOUTS

You may already be making up your own workouts at this point. If not, however, I have the following tips for you:

1. Schedule abdominal training first in your routine as a whole-body warm up.

2. Never do calf work before Squats (it'll cause your legs to vibrate excessively while squatting).

3. Do forearm work last in your routine (it will pump up your forearms so much that it'll be difficult to grasp anything for the next 20–30 minutes).

4. Never do arm training before your torso workout. Most pec, delt, and lat exercises also involve the arms, and normally your arms will give out first when doing Benches, Militaries, and Rows. There's no use aggravating this already bad situation by further weakening your arms through training them first.

5. Try to work your larger muscle groups early in your training

bodybuilding routines

sessions. They require a huge energy expenditure that might be difficult to muster up when you are fatigued late in a workout.

Other than following these five rules, you should always attempt to do your most underdeveloped muscle groups first in your routine. This technique is called *muscle priority training,* and it's the best way to bring up a lagging body part. It's only at the beginning of a workout—when your physical and mental energies are at a peak—that you can train a weak muscle group with maximum intensity. Later in your training session you will probably be too tired to train with peak intensity.

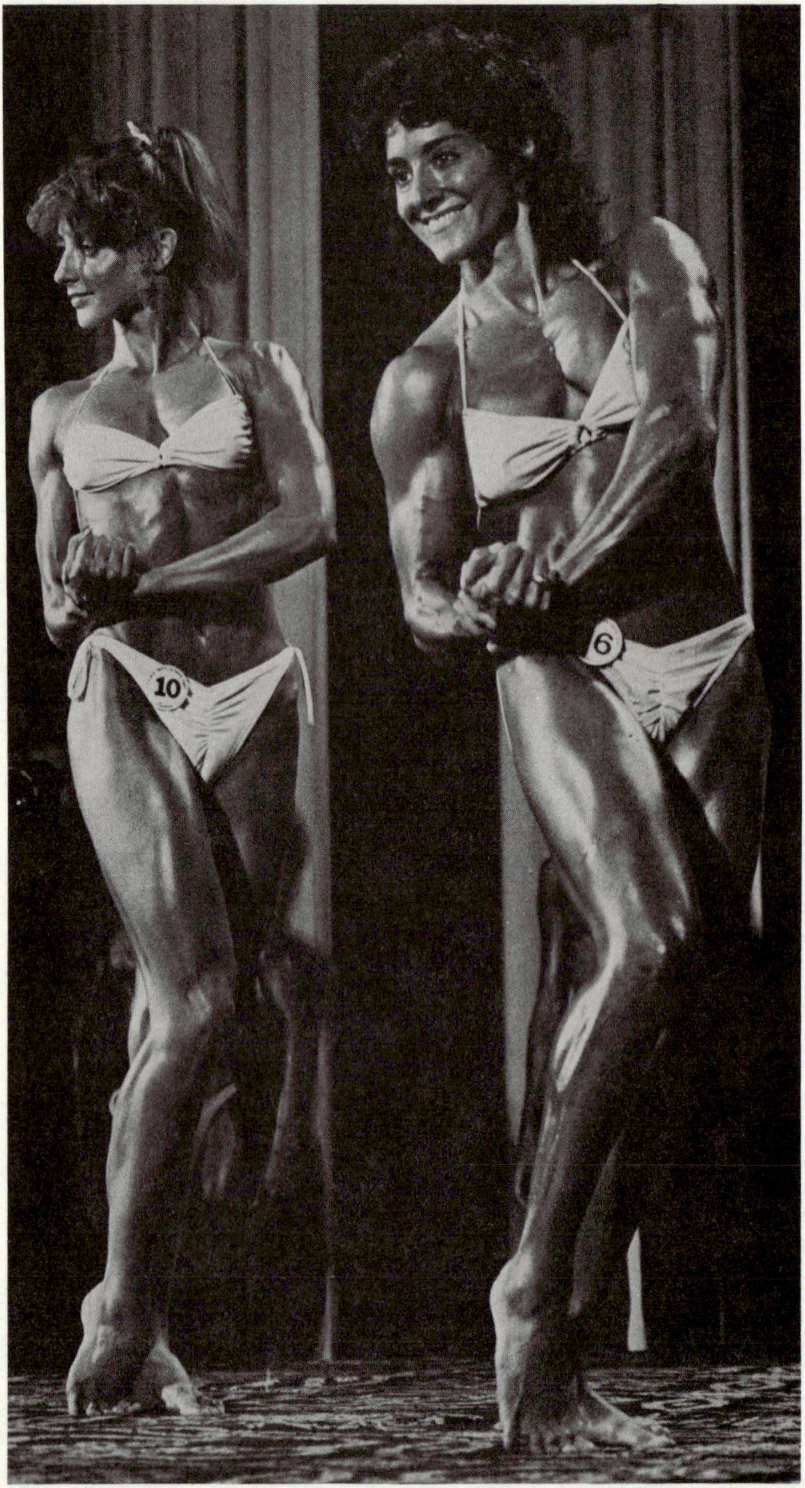
10
6

chapter ten
competitive techniques

Once you firmly decide to compete, you must systematically prepare yourself to peak exactly on the day of your competition. This is not an easy task to accomplish, however, and it usually takes several peaking attempts to learn how to correctly time a peak.

Take written and (if possible) photographic notes of exactly how your body responds to various exercise and dietary stimuli each time you attempt to peak. Then, using these notes, you can evaluate your physique at one-week intervals for the final six weeks of your contest countdown, and daily for the last week. If you are a little too fat at one checkpoint, you can tighten your diet and/or increase your aerobic activity to get back on schedule. Or, if you're getting lean-looking too quickly, you can retard your peak a bit by eating more calories for a day or two.

The information presented in this chapter will help you to prepare optimally for your first contest, or—for more experienced competitors—reach a higher peak of condition than ever before. I will discuss: how to learn competitive practices by watching a competition; posing; contest grooming; low-fat vs. low-carbohydrate dieting; how to train around injuries; mental aspects of bodybuilding; training intensification techniques; double-split routines; aerobic exercise; and bodybuilding pharmacology.

LEARN BY WATCHING

It would be folly to enter a competition without first having seen several, because you can learn so much about competing from carefully observing a bodybuilding show. You will learn more about posing, how a competition is judged, and what posing suit styles and hair styles are most popular. You will also be able to evaluate your current level of development by comparing how you look to how the contestants in a show appear.

Women's bodybuilding competitions are held all over America and Canada, as well as over the rest of the globe. They are commonly announced well ahead of time in the various bodybuilding magazines, as well as through posters on gym walls. Once you have competed, you will be included on a mailing list held by a District Representative, and show promoters will send you announcements of upcoming events well in advance.

As soon as you notice that a competition will be held in your area, buy tickets well in advance. The longer you wait to purchase tickets, the further back you will sit in the auditorium and the worse your view of the contest. Virtually all competitions are now prejudged, usually in the morning or early afternoon of the show, and it's vital that you attend the prejudging, since that's where most of the action takes place.

Because of continuing controversy regarding the point system used in bodybuilding contests, the AFWB and the IFBB adopted the placement system in the fall of 1982. In the first three major rounds, each focusing on different aspects of physique, seven judges rank all contestants first, second, third, etc. For example,

competitive techniques

if all seven judges ranked one contestant first, she would receive *five* points—her highest and lowest placements (being the same in such a rare case) would be eliminated to ensure fairness. After three rounds, the six contestants with the lowest scores are chosen to compete in a posedown round; all other contestants are ranked according to lowest scores and those placements are final.

In the posedown round, each judge picks his or her ranking of the finalists, first through sixth. Each score counts in this round, so the minimum amount of points is 7 and the maximum is 42. These totals are added to those of the first three rounds and the final rankings are determined by lowest scores.

As you sit at the prejudging, try to get a good general impression of the competitive atmosphere. How well-developed are the women? What posing suits do they wear? What colors? How much makeup do they have on? How do they style their hair? When are they or aren't they most aggressive? How do they stand in the lineup when not actually being judged? How much oil do they use? How do they pose? When do they smile? Through careful observation of several shows you can answer these—and many other—questions and be much better prepared for everything you encounter when you do step on stage for the first time. Even then, you'll never stop learning new things about competing more effectively.

Observe carefully how each of the three posing rounds is conducted. In Round I the contestants are judged standing "relaxed" facing the judges, with left sides toward the panel, with backs to the judges and with right sides toward the panel. This round primarily reveals body symmetry, proportional balance, and general muscle tone and development.

Round II consists of a series of compulsory poses designed to assess a bodybuilder's overall development and muscularity under more or less equal conditions. Notice especially how each bodybuilder adapts and interprets a compulsory pose to best display her own physique. These compulsory poses are periodically changed, so observe them in several contests and practice the stances carefully before competing.

Depictions of the current compulsory poses—as well as written

Relaxed poses—Kike Elomaa (1981 Miss Olympia) and Laura compare front poses.

Relaxed back pose.

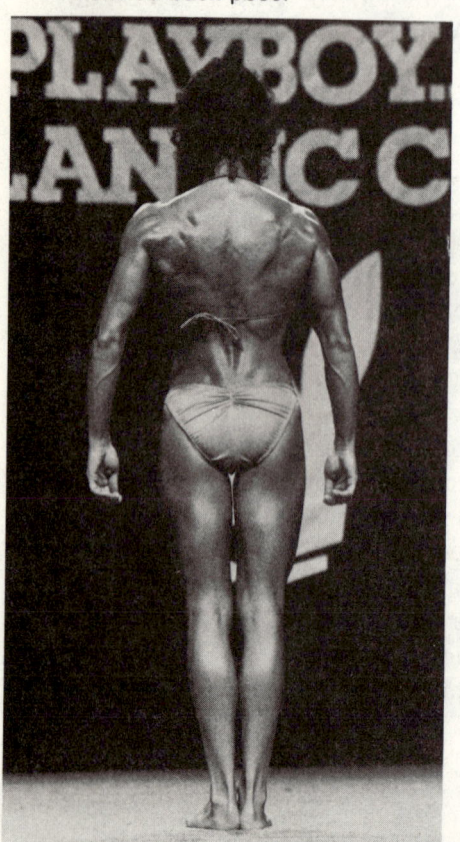

Relaxed right side pose.

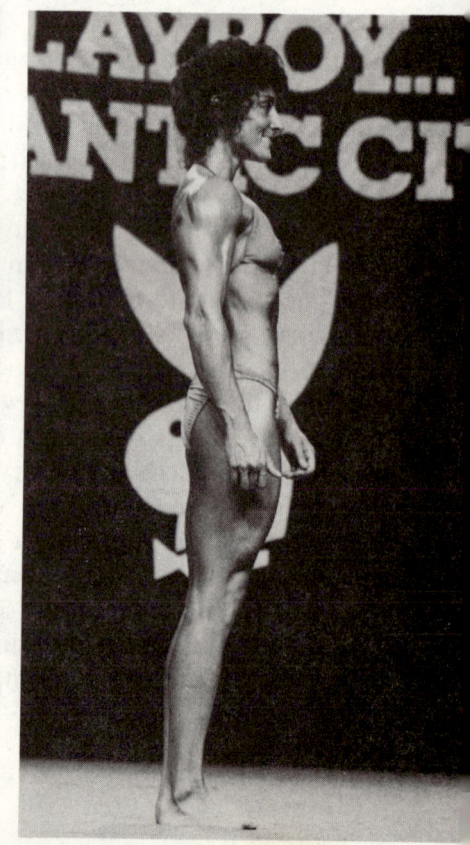

Compulsory pose, Round II—front double biceps.

rules for performing each one—are included in the AFWB Judging Guide. This booklet is available for $2.00 from the American Federation of Women Bodybuilders, Box 937, Riverview, FL 33569. Having this Judging Guide is a must for all competitive bodybuilders.

In Rounds I and II the judges will observe each contestant individually in the appropriate poses, then in small groups to compare one athlete against another. These comparisons can take considerable time to complete, but they are necessary to objectively judge a competition. Indeed, no judge records a round score until all of these comparisons have been made.

Compulsory pose, Round II—side chest.

competitive techniques

Compulsory pose, Round II—back double biceps.

Compulsory pose, Round II—side triceps.

competitive techniques

Compulsory pose, Round II—abs and legs.

Round III consists of individual free-posing to music, and no comparisons are made in the round. I will discuss posing for this round in detail in the next section of this chapter. After reading that section, you will have a full appreciation for how uniquely individual each woman's free-posing routine is. It's an expression of her own unique personality, as your own must become before you compete.

Most bodybuilding shows feature guest posers, who are the superstars of the sport. Many show promoters have at least one woman guest poser, and you should pay special attention to her routine. Unless it is close to one of her own competitions, she won't be in peak condition, but she will still pose masterfully. Watching her move gracefully and powerfully through her routine should inspire you and further educate you in the art of posing.

The final thing I would like you to note at each contest is the total elation of the winner(s). One day you will be up there receiving your own trophy, and that momentary thrill of victory will make all of the hours you spend in the gym well worth the effort!

POSING

To me, contest posing is a euphoric and charismatic extension of my unique personality. When it's clicking and I've developed a rapport with my audience, nothing can compare with being onstage in top condition!

Working on my posing is just as important to me as training any body part. And, it's a shame that more women bodybuilders don't work as seriously on their posing as I do. They slave away for hundreds of hours in the gym, do as much aerobic training as an aspiring marathon runner, and starve themselves unmercifully. They end up in superb bodybuilding condition, but in competition they don't place nearly as high as they should.

Many well-developed women lose because their posing is inept and ineffective. I've seen dozens of bodybuilders pick out their music two days before a contest, then throw together a routine at

"In my posing routine I always include both esthetic open-handed poses and harder closed-fist shots. Variety is very important when planning a winning free-posing routine."

123

the last minute. They end up looking clumsy and amateurish onstage, and often they are defeated by a bodybuilder with noticeably inferior development who has a better posing routine.

In contrast, I—as do most professional women bodybuilders—know what music I will use and which poses I will do many months prior to competing. Throughout the year I spend at least 30-60 minutes per day practicing my posing, and close to a contest I may practice twice as much.

The extra posing not only makes my routine more smooth, but also improves my muscle hardness. If I'm too keyed up and can't sleep at night during the week before a Miss Olympia show—and many bodybuilders share this problem—I jump out of bed and practice my posing routine until I'm exhausted enough to doze off.

To become a great poser, you must start with the philosophy that posing is crucial to all bodybuilders. In Chapter 2 I mentioned that I modeled my first routine after that of Ed Corney, and he once stated my premise perfectly when he wrote, "Only by extending your personality through effective and dramatic posing can you let the judges and audience identify with you and know exactly what you've gone through to reach the top. Add great posing to years in the gym and months on a tight diet, and you're sure to carry home some new trophies."

This is precisely the posing philosophy I follow. My posing is my means of self-expression as a bodybuilder and an extension of my unique personality. Of course, if you try to imitate someone else's style, it will hurt your overall contest presentation. You have to develop your own personal style and combine it with music that suits you perfectly. Only in this manner can you stand onstage, develop a communication link with your audience, and tell them with your body how enthusiastic you feel about being a bodybuilder.

A novice woman bodybuilder has a natural tendency to try a few shots in front of a mirror as soon as her body begins to improve. This is a good starting point, because you must totally master at least 10-12 good individual poses before you can hope

competitive techniques

to construct a free-posing routine. Pro bodybuilders might do 25-30 great poses, but in the beginning it's much better for you to have 10 poses in which you look very good than to knock out 20 that do little to highlight your hard-earned physique.

Look at every pose of every woman bodybuilder that you see in the various bodybuilding magazines. Attmpt to duplicate those poses that appeal to you the most, but don't expect to get any of them right the first time. Every bodybuilder does standard poses a little differently. You'll need to experiment continually with new foot stances, hand positions, slight twists of your torso, and so on until you have adapted a pose to suit your own physique perfectly.

Posing is an art form. Along with full body control, you must have head, eye, and facial control. For every pose you must know exactly how you want to position your head and where you want to look. Too many women practice constantly in front of a mirror, and as a result they look straight ahead on every pose. Without the mirror as their focus—as is the case at a contest—the bodybuilder appears confused about how her poses look and seems unsure of herself.

Go ahead and practice with a mirror until you have each pose down pat, but then work without the mirror. Have a friend take Polaroid photos of each pose to be sure you are still hitting it perfectly.

One of the toughest skills to master is remembering to flex every muscle group in each pose. Frequently even experienced women flex their upper bodies to the limit in a pose, but totally forget to tense all of their leg muscles. That looks very amateurish, and it's a problem you should conquer in practice before considering competition.

Smile, if you wish, as you pose. Nothing is as exciting to a bodybuilding audience as a competitor breaking into a big smile when they've applauded particularly enthusiastically for one of her best poses.

If you don't feel comfortable smiling, adopt an expression that looks relaxed. Relaxing your face while tensing every other

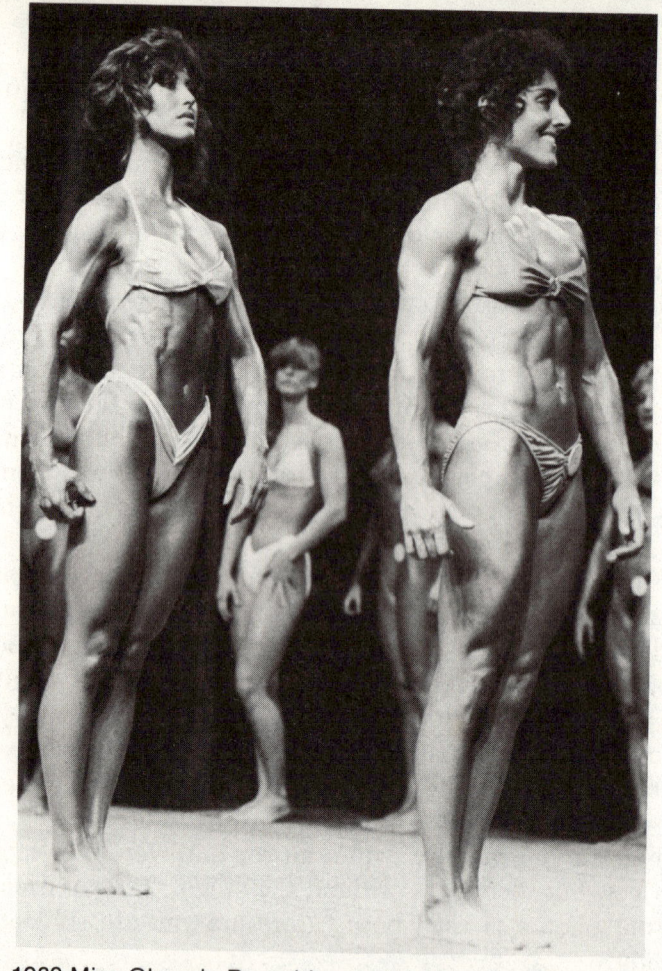

1982 Miss Olympia Round I comparison of Rachel McLish (the eventual winner) and Laura (who placed sixth).

muscle in your body is akin to patting your head and rubbing your stomach at the same time. It takes plenty of practice, but the ability *can* be mastered.

I practice posing under strong, harsh light because I don't want to delude myself about weaknesses in my physique. I also use two full-length mirrors so I can view my straight-back poses as clearly as would a contest judge.

Some bodybuilders choose poses that hide their weak points, but I prefer to eliminate weaknesses by training those body parts more intensely. Learn to recognize your weak body parts as you

competitive techniques

practice posing. Hiding them with tricky poses isn't nearly as good as pinpointing the weak areas and bombing them with heavy exercise until they are up to par.

Several months before you plan to compete, you should begin regularly practicing the four facing poses of Round I in the IFBB/AFWB judging system, as well as the compulsory poses of Round II. Even though in Round I you are standing "relaxed"—showing the front, back, and both sides of your body to the judges—these poses still require practice. Tiny shifts of the arms, legs, or torso can significantly improve each of these stances. And a look of total confidence and control also helps. Since Round I counts for a third of the total score, only a fool would neglect practicing these four stances.

As you work on the compulsory poses in Round II (which also count for a third of your total score) learn to hold each one for at least 30 seconds. Sometimes during the prejudging—usually when comparisons are being made—you will have to hold your compulsory poses for 30–40 seconds, *and* without shaking like a leaf. Holding these poses so long in practice will help you to master control of both your muscles and breathing patterns.

In my free-posing routine (Round III, which counts for the final third of a bodybuilder's score), I want all of my poses to be unique. When I do a twisting back shot, for example, I want it to be different from the same basic pose done by every other bodybuilder. So, I work on it and work on it until it *is* unique.

I like to combine clenched-fist and open-handed positions in my routine. The audience responds more boisterously to clenched fists, but the open-handed poses have greater flair and esthetic appeal. Mixing the two is very effective, and I've always included some clenched-fist poses in my routine.

In my free-posing routine I am also careful to use a wide variety of leg positions, including lunging and kneeling stances. To my way of thinking, the more variety you present in your routine, the better. Still, I see many women competitors using only two or three basic leg stances to display 20–30 upper body positions. Why forget your legs?

I like to look at every possible photo taken of myself onstage.

1982 Miss Olympia Round I comparison of Shelley Gruwell ('81 World Grand Prix Champion) and Laura.

1982 Miss Olympia Round I comparison of Carla Dunlap (Laura's successor in the American Women's Bodybuilding Championship) and Laura.

competitive techniques

Every time I see a photo of myself I can spot something, however minor it may be, that needs changing in a pose. And when someone suggests an alteration of a pose, I'll try it in practice. If it doesn't work precisely right, I'll play with it in a wide variety of other forms before I'll ever consider abandoning the idea.

Long before I formulate my free-posing routine each year, I will have chosen music that is an expression of my personality. If your musical selection isn't arranged exactly as you'd like it, you'll need to learn to splice tapes together to achieve the effect you're after. You will be onstage free-posing for only two or three minutes, so your music has to be right.

Posing must be choreographed to the music, and many bodybuilders use a professional dance choreographer to achieve this. Each pose should be synchronized with the flow of the music and poses are best synchronized with musical crescendos.

I prefer to pose to music without a vocal track. When the music has vocals, the audience tends to think I should be synchronizing my poses with the words rather than with the music. To me that is sort of schizophrenic and detracts from the impact of my routine.

As you develop a posing routine, pay attention to your transitions between poses. Locking in each pose tells the judges what they need to know, while the transitions are your best means of self-expression. Generally, your eyes should follow the motion of your hands, and you should take a shallow breath or two out and in during your transition. Be careful to hold your stomach in as you do this, however! Then hold your breath while you have your actual pose locked into position.

You can use a choreographer to good advantage in devising transitions between poses. Many of the better women posers have extensive dance or gymnastics backgrounds, which is a great advantage when working on posing transitions. And the more competitions you watch, the more ideas you'll come up with for uniquely individual movements between poses.

I hold each individual pose for approximately four seconds, which gives the judges and audience plenty of time to evaluate my physique. I've arrived at this four-second figure by timing the

"While I personally prefer to present a hard, pure bodybuilding appearance, it's sometimes enjoyable to have my hair styled differently and my face made up for softer and more glamorous photos." *(Bob Gardner)*

competitive techniques

scene cuts in television commercials. These commercials are put together by experts seeking maximum mental impact, and the cuts from scene to scene are usually about four seconds apart.

As you near full preparation of your free-posing routine, a video camera and recorder can be a great help. With one you can tape and view your entire routine, complete with its accompanying music. From the videotape you can spot any tiny errors in poses or timing and still have sufficient time to correct them.

The final type of posing takes place in the posedown, and you should practice a quick and aggressive routine for that point in your competition. If two bodybuilders are equally developed, it will usually be the more aggressive one who will receive the majority of judges' votes.

Once you have fully prepared your posing routine, all that's left is to step confidently onstage and develop a camaraderie with your audience. Most audiences like the heavy muscular shots, so I reward them toward the end of my routine by slamming out several such poses, one after another, like the end of a fireworks display.

If the audience reacts with loud applause and cheers to one of my poses, I always respond with my biggest smile. I can't help smiling because it's such an incredible high when the audience appreciates my efforts. And that's the essence of why I am a bodybuilder!

PERSONAL APPEARANCE

In addition to your muscular development, there are several personal appearance factors that can help you to win your next competition. Among these are hairstyle, makeup, posing attire, tan (if appropriate), and body oil.

AFWB/IFBB rules dictate that a woman's hairstyle must be worn up so it won't obscure the development of her upper back and shoulders. Within the scope of this ruling, you have several options. I've always worn my hair in a soft and full perm for competitions, and only occasionally have pinned it up and back for photo sessions. Lisa Elliott has adopted an even softer perm that complements her facial features perfectly.

Short hair presents no style problems, while long, straight hair is the hardest to style. Most successful women bodybuilders with long hair wear it pinned up either in the back or off to one side. Long hair can also be braided and the braids arranged on the head, as long as the resulting styling isn't too harsh looking.

Like stage actors and actresses, women bodybuilders should wear heavier makeup onstage than under more normal circumstances. The stage lights at a competition are quite bright and they tend to wash out normally applied makeup. It's difficult to tell exactly how much makeup to apply, because that can vary widely according to a woman's facial features and coloring. Your best bet will be to experiment with various degrees of makeup and have a friend evaluate it for you while you're onstage competing.

Jewelry should be kept to an absolute minimum onstage. I wear only tiny earrings and a thin chain around my neck with a small medallion that has great meaning to me. Heavy bracelets and necklaces, watches, waist and ankle chains, and ostentatious rings or earrings can distract a judge from the important job of evaluating your physique.

Your posing attire should be chosen to provide minimum distraction as well, plus to display your hard-earned physique to its best advantage. Never wear a patterned suit. Instead, choose one that is of a solid color that harmonizes with your own coloring. I personally perfer various shades of blue, particularly turquoise, but I've seen virtually every color in the rainbow on top women bodybuilders. And, in the past I've worn a number of other colors.

The cut of a posing suit should reveal upper thigh, lower abdominal, pectoral, and back development to the fullest. And the suit can't be allowed to ride up or down your body as you pose (sometimes double-sided tape can eliminate this problem). The only way to find if a suit is the correct size and cut is to visit every possible beach wear shop and try on all of their suits. It's also a very good idea to take at least two suits with you to each

Photo by Bob Gardner.

competition. The one you wear at the prejudging can often become so spotted with oil as to be useless for the evening show.

Fair-skinned bodybuilders *must* get a tan, since a darker skin reveals underlying muscles in the boldest relief. A natural tan is best, because the sun helps to draw water from your body and thin your skin. Begin sunbathing at least six weeks before your competition, so you can avoid a skin-bloating sunburn.

For winter competitions and at other times when you can't get a deep natural tan, you can use an artificial tanning agent or skin makeup. I strongly suggest that you use a makeup product called Indian Earth, which is available at most cosmetic counters. Indian Earth is a powder that can be rubbed on your skin to give you a deep, mahogany-colored tan. It doesn't come off on your warmup suit if it's rubbed on hard, you can apply oil over it, and Indian Earth washes off completely with a good shower.

All bodybuilders use body oil to highlight their muscularity. It's best to use a moderate amount of a vegetable oil that will soak into your pores and slowly reappear as you warm up, giving your skin a "glow" instead of a sheen. Almond and avocado oil are very good for this purpose, but virtually all vegetable oils work well as long as you apply the oil evenly all over your body. Avoid petroleum-based mineral oils, which lie on your skin and make it look like someone bundled you in plastic freezer wrapping.

PRECONTEST DIET

There are two popular types of precontest diets used by women bodybuilders. One of these is a low-fat/low-calorie regimen and the other is a low-carbohydrate diet. In my own precontest dieting phase, I actually follow a diet low in both calories and carbohydrates.

More women these days seem to prefer using a low-fat diet, because it allows one to consume enough carbohydrates to keep training energy levels fairly high. The key to this diet lies in the fact that fats are more than twice as high in calories as an equivalent weight of protein or carbohydrate. When metabolized in the body for energy, one gram of fat yields nine calories, compared to only four calories for a gram of either protein or carbohydrate.

By avoiding high-fat foods and replacing them with protein and carbohydrates, you automatically lower your caloric intake. For every deficit of 3,500 calories you can create below your daily caloric maintenance level, you will lose one pound of body fat. And, crucially, you can lose fat without losing much muscle mass, as is often the case on a low-carb diet.

The weakness in low-fat diets is that carbohydrate foods retain water in your body at a rate of four grams of water per gram of carbohydrate. As a result, many women who follow a low-fat diet are able to drastically reduce their body fat levels, but can still end up looking smooth and bloated from the water retained by carbs eaten prior to competition.

Here is a three-meal-per-day, sample menu for low-fat dieting (amounts of these items are at your discretion):

Breakfast—egg whites, bran cereal with non-fat milk, one piece of fruit, and coffee.

Lunch—tuna (no dressing), lettuce salad (with vinegar only as a dressing), baked potato (no butter or sour cream), and iced tea with lemon.

Dinner—broiled chicken breast (no skin), brown rice, salad, piece of fruit, and coffee.

competitive techniques

While a low-carbohydrate diet will allow you to really rip up your physique—particularly in terms of reducing water retention in the body—it is an uncomfortable regimen to follow and it usually results in lost muscle mass. Since your brain craves a normal level of blood sugar and can't get it when you are avoiding carbohydrates, you can be very irritable and become easily depressed when on a low-carb diet.

To avoid confusion, here is a sample one-day menu for low-carbohydrate dieting:

Breakfast—eggs, steak, and coffee (with cream and artificial sweetener).
Lunch—roast turkey, salad (with no-carb dressing, which can be high in fat content), and iced tea (with artificial sweetener).
Dinner—roast beef, cheese, salad, and coffee.

I can achieve peak contest condition only if I follow a combination of low-fat and low-carb dieting. For a long period of time I follow the low-fat diet—also being careful to limit my dietary intake of sodium, which holds large quantities of water in the body—in order to reduce my body fat to a very low level.

Then for about a week I try to go to zero carbohydrate intake, which flushes all excess water from my body. Finally, the night before competing I eat 80–100 grams of low-bulk carbohydrate food (such as dried fruit) to restore glycogen to my muscles and fill them out, as well as to increase my vascularity. Under 100 grams of carbohydrate intake and I look my best onstage, while more than 100 grams begins to retain water under my skin rather than in my muscles, smoothing me out and ruining my perfectly defined appearance.

TRAINING AROUND INJURIES

To a degree, the progress you make as a competitive bodybuilder depends on how successfully you avoid training injuries and how well you are able to train around those injuries you do incur. By thoroughly warming up your muscles before using heavy training poundages, keeping warm throughout the workout and maintaining proper biomechanics when doing exercises, you can effectively avoid most injuries.

If you are injured, search for exercises that allow you to train the rest of your body without causing pain or additional harm to the injured joint or muscle. In the case of a lower back injury, this can tend to be somewhat difficult, but you can find exercises that can be done lying down and still work each muscle group fairly hard. With most other injuries, however, you can usually find exercises that will allow you to train heavily without aggravating an existing injury.

After your injury has healed, you can resume normal training without having allowed yourself to get out of shape while injured. You *could* take a layoff from training whenever you are injured, but every missed workout could put an opponent who doesn't miss hers further ahead of you. So, whenever possible, train around injuries until they have healed enough to resume normal full-body workout sessions.

MENTAL APPROACH

The human mind, if correctly utilized, is phenomenally powerful. It has literally moved mountains, sent men to the moon, fostered great civilizations, and developed a generation of bodybuilders who would have blown the minds of iron game cognoscenti only a decade or two ago.

Yes, you have within yourself a power that can turn you into a superb bodybuilder **if** you can learn to use it effectively. But how can you harness that incredible power for your own self-improvement? In this section I will tell you the answer to that question, allowing you to reach your unique bodybuilding goals more speedily.

At my bodybuilding seminars I am frequently asked how much of my success can be attributed to my mental approach to the sport. I always answer that 100% of my success depends on my mind, because the mind is the potentate in bodybuilding. I can—

competitive techniques

and have—dieted and trained optimally for a competition but not appeared onstage in peak condition, because my mind wasn't fully into it. Unless the mind triggers off the ability to improve and peak, all of the training and strict dieting in the world will go for naught.

If you're not properly psyched up—that is, if you don't have the will to win—you simply won't be able to endure the grueling training and strict diet it takes to win a high-level bodybuilding title. I've been a winner in bodybuilding and several other sports, and I definitely like the feeling. I know that when I am doing absolutely everything I can in my workouts and am strictly adhering to my precontest diet, I *will* win.

Two months before I won the American Championships in 1980 I wrote in my training diary, "If you want to become the American Champion you must reach deep within yourself to bring out that will to win that can only come from yourself. You must deny yourself lesser desires and pleasures to strive for what is most important to you. With these things in mind, you alone can determine your fate. With these things accomplished, the victory will be yours and yours alone."

I did reach deeply enough for that special will to win. As I trained to win the America I knew that no one in her right mind would have pushed as hard as I was, so I was totally sure that I would win. I willingly tortured myself in the gym each day in order to reach my goal.

Bodybuilding is an exacting task master. It doesn't allow the weak of will to win. There is no room among the sport's great champions for one without a burning desire to succeed against all odds, to strive with the fabled last ounce of courage to reach a cherished goal.

The effort of properly preparing to win a contest just isn't worth it unless you actually improve from competition to competition. It takes all of my will power, self-discipline, desire, and courage to prepare to win, and it's not easy to make such an investment merely to take home a trophy for second or third place. (Actually, circumstances beyond your control may prevent

"Pumping up backstage prior to the 1980 Ms. America prejudging, I was supremely confident. In my mind, I had already won the title hundreds of times."
(Bill Dobbins)

you from winning, but as long as you improve each contest you *have* won!) I focus totally on a coming competition, sacrificing my social life and everything else that mortal women consider important in order to appear at my best onstage.

If you're not capable of putting forth your best effort, you're better off staying out of competition until you *are* capable of doing so. Anything less than your best effort isn't good enough. You might place fairly well in a contest on less than 100% effort, but you won't win.

So, developing the will to win, the will to achieve greatness, is the first step in achieving a winning mental approach to bodybuilding. Without it, you will be condemned to the ranks of also-rans and almost-weres. Do you want more than anything else in life to succeed as a bodybuilder? If you do, you are on your way to the top.

Imagining how you will soon look is your next step to establishing a good mental approach to bodybuilding, because this is the starting point to using the visualization technique to improve your physique. When I first committed myself to bodybuilding, I

competitive techniques

established a mental image of how I wanted to look eventually as a bodybuilder. And over the years, despite many assaults by judges and other bodybuilding officials on this image, I have maintained it exactly as I first conceptualized it.

My personal preference is to be massive, muscular, and hard-looking. I've been muscular almost all of my life, and that's what I feel most comfortable with. That is me, and I can't be something I'm not. I think I would dislike myself if I compromised my standards.

Femininity can be either soft or hard. My first love is to be as massive as possible and very muscular, but I'm not going to confine myself totally to that image. I want to achieve physical balance and at the same time to achieve an esthetic overall appearance. Women can and should have muscle mass and look muscular if they are going to call themselves bodybuilders. Let's face it—anyone can be big and overweight, and anyone can be small and lean; the object of bodybuilding is to be big and lean at the same time.

Regardless of the course women's bodybuilding judging takes, I'm going to stick to my guns and come into a contest looking like what *I* feel a bodybuilder should appear. Pressure from the public, as well as internal pressures from bodybuilding officials, won't dissuade me from achieving this goal. I may change my appearance from the neck up (e.g., hairstyle and facial makeup) for a contest in the future, but from the neck down I will be a *bodybuilder.*

The point I'm trying to make is that *you* must also stick to your guns once you decide what you want to look like. I'm not, however, trying to influence you in choosing the type of body you'd like to attain. Femininity, as I said, can be either soft or hard, and the choice is yours. Once you make it, however, stick with it. It doesn't matter what someone else likes, because you alone have to live with your body. Go for what *you* like.

As you develop your image of future physical perfection, make it as vivid and realistic as possible. See absolutely every detail of muscular development when you close your eyes—every vein, every mound of muscle, and every cut in your body. Your image

Visualization also means looking at yourself in the mirror and seeing what's not there . . . yet.

should be so vividly realistic that it's almost like a film image projected against the insides of your eyelids.

Once you have this image firmly established, you can use it to program your powerful subconscious mind to assist you in attaining your goals. Once your subconscious mind is properly programmed it can help you to avoid eating junk foods, avoid missing training sessions, and be totally committed to what you are doing with no discomfort whatsoever. With a properly programmed subconscious mind, bodybuilding training and diet become a joy rather than something to be endured.

Visualization is an operative form of what psychologists call *self-actualization*. If you can imagine yourself as becoming something and make your imagination realistic enough over a long enough period of time, you will actualize this imagined persona. You've probably seen women who have dreamed all of their lives about being a nurse, a pilot, or whatever, and they easily reach their goals. They do so through self-actualization, or through an unconscious application of the visualization process.

To consciously visualize, set aside 15 or 20 minutes each night

competitive techniques

before you fall asleep in which to practice visualization. Simply lie relaxed and conjure up your image of future physical perfection. Lie there enjoying this image for several minutes, and then go to sleep. Doing this regularly will program your mind quite effectively. It's almost like *creative daydreaming*. No doubt this sounds fairly simplistic to you, but it definitely works well for a bodybuilder, or for any other athlete.

Be certain, as you acquire your image of future perfection, that you keep it realistic. The reason I began competing in bodybuilding is that I had hit a wall in my water skiing. I was shorter than most of the really successful women skiers and slaloming as well as any short person could. Since they progressively shorten the rope each pass in the slalom, however, height and reach make a big difference.

After eight years as a skier, I knew I couldn't go any farther in the sport. Even if I had used visualization every night, I would have been stuck where I was. I wasn't going to grow any taller or lengthen my arms. So, I had to be realistic and move on to another sport for which I had more natural talent. That proved—somewhat by chance—to be bodybuilding.

The more you visualize, the better you will become at it. Eventually, you will be able to actually feel what it's like in competition almost to the point where you can smell the oil on your body. You can even feel what it's like to be living inside a greatly improved body and what it's like to win. When you get to this point, you are a sure winner.

At the America in 1980, I had visualized my victory so many times and so completely that I just couldn't wait to get onstage to actualize my triumph. I knew I was the best and this gave me the body language of a winner onstage. If you go to enough bodybuilding competitions, you'll no doubt notice women with this type of body language, as well as women who simply look like losers the second they step onstage, even though they may have very good development.

Some champion bodybuilders periodically update their mental images, but I've stuck with the same one over the years. The only change has been in my physique as I come closer and closer to reaching this image. I look for improvements in my weaker areas as short-range goals, but I'm after my big, pie-in-the-sky, long-term goal, which is ultimately achieving the image I have set for myself.

My final mental bodybuilding technique is to ask myself motivation-improving questions each day. Do you want to reach a new level of personal excellence? Are you willing to pay the price? Will you sacrifice anything to reach your goals? Answering "yes" isn't enough. You can't fool yourself when you ask these questions, because bodybuilding takes genuine commitment and effort. Unfortunately, many women bodybuilders lie to themselves. You know from looking at them that they're not doing what they say they are, because they would look much better if they were. So, you have to be truthful to yourself. See your weak points, and do something about them.

If you use the mental techniques I've outlined in this section, you can one day be a much better person. You can unlock the sleeping giant within yourself and reach the moon as a bodybuilder!

TRAINING INTENSIFICATION

There are a wide variety of training intensification techniques that you can use during a precontest cycle—as well as during the off-season in some cases—to achieve a higher peak. In this section, I will discuss the eight intensification techniques that I personally use most frequently—training to failure, cheating, forced reps, quality training, supersets and trisets, peak contraction, continuous tension, and iso-tension posing contraction. You should experiment with each of these techniques and use your training instinct to determine which should ultimately be included in your bodybuilding philosophy.

Training to Failure

The more deeply you get into bodybuilding, the more frequently you should push a set to failure, or to the point where your

"Intensity is the name of the game in building large, high-quality muscles. No pain, no gain!" *(Bill Dobbins)*

muscles have momentarily become so fatigued that you can't complete a repetition, regardless of how hard you try. I personally push virtually every set I do (other than warm-ups) to the point of failure—and even beyond failure—in order to give my muscles an intense growth stimulation.

Most novice bodybuilders train to failure on only one or two sets per muscle group, and this limits the amount of muscle mass they can acquire. So, you should gradually push more and more of your sets to failure, and ultimately use cheating reps and forced reps to actually push past the point of normal muscular failure. Only then will you be able to develop huge, high-quality muscles.

Cheating

Beginning and intermediate bodybuilders are always cautioned to do their exercises in strict form, because they almost always cheat to make an exercise easier to do. Advanced bodybuilders, however, use cheating form to actually make an exercise harder to do, and thus make it more productive in terms of developing additional muscle mass and quality.

Once you have gone to failure in an exercise, you can cheat intelligently to push your muscles past the point of normal failure and thus stress your muscles more intensely than is normally possible. This is accomplished by using only enough extraneous body movement to get your barbell, dumbbell, or dumbbells (it's very difficult to cheat using machines) past the sticking point at which your fatigued muscles have failed to move the bar any higher.

Let's use the Barbell Curl as an example of how to correctly use cheating to push your biceps past the point of normal failure. Using 85 pounds, you do seven or eight Curls in strict form until you are unable to move the barbell completely upward. Only *then* can you use just enough body swing to accelerate the barbell past the sticking point from where you finish the rep using *only* your own biceps strength. Finally, you slowly lower the barbell back to the starting point, resisting the lowering motion very strongly with your dwindling biceps strength.

Since your biceps will fatigue very quickly, you must swing the barbell a little harder to get it up on each succeeding repetition. Ordinarily, you won't need to do more than two or three cheating reps. And, very few bodybuilders can profit from doing more than one or two cheating sets per muscle group each time the group is trained.

Forced Reps

Forced reps are the second way that I push my working muscles past the point of failure. This technique involves first going to the

competitive techniques

point of failure, then having a training partner assist you to complete two or three reps past the failure point.

When I fail the seventh repetition after doing six strict reps with 100 pounds in a Barbell Curl, that only means that my biceps muscles have become too fatigued to handle 100 pounds for another repetition. But they are undoubtedly still strong enough to curl 90-95 pounds for another rep and perhaps 85-90 pounds for yet another.

The easiest way to progressively lighten a barbell to force out two or three reps past the normal point of failure is to have your training partner pull up on the bar *just enough* so your fatigue-weakened muscles can complete each succeeding forced rep. In the case of my Barbell Curls, my partner would pull up with only 5-10 pounds of pressure for the first forced rep, 10-15 pounds for the second, and 15-20 for the third.

It's important when you do forced reps that you lower the barbell under your own power while strongly resisting its downward pressure. Or, to make a rep even more intense, you can have your partner actually add resistance to the bar as it moves downward, forcing you to work even harder to resist its downward momentum.

Quality Training

To achieve peak muscularity for a competition, it is necessary to quality train, which involves progressively shortening the length of rest intervals between sets. In the off-season I will rest approximately 60 seconds between sets, while close to a contest my rest intervals will average only 15-20 seconds.

The faster training allows you to do more work in a set period of time, which greatly intensifies your training and helps to bring out maximum muscularity. In combination with aerobic training and a strict precontest diet, quality training with the heaviest possible weights allows me to become extremely muscular for a competition while retaining the greatest possible degree of muscle mass.

Supersets and Trisets

One way to quality train is to superset or triset your exercises. Supersets involve doing two exercises with no rest between movements, then taking a rest interval between supersets. Trisets are similar groupings of three movements. Because you take no rest between the exercises in a superset or triset, using these techniques helps to reduce the average rest interval between sets.

The simplest form of superset is done between antagonistic muscle groups, such as biceps + triceps, or quadriceps + hamstrings. Here are examples of three such supersets:

Biceps + Triceps = Barbell Curls + Lying Triceps Extensions
Quads + Hamstrings = Leg Extensions + Leg Curls
Lats + Pectorals = Lat Pulldowns + Bench Presses

If you wish to make your training even more intense, you should do supersets consisting of two exercises for *one* muscle group. Here are several examples of such a superset:

Thighs = Leg Extensions + Squats
Pecs = Bench Presses + Flyes
Lats = Chins + Seated Pulley Rowing
Calves = Standing Calf Raises + Seated Calf Raises
Delts = Presses Behind Neck + Side Laterals
Biceps = Preacher Curls + Standing Barbell Curls
Triceps = Lying Triceps Extensions + Pulley Pushdowns

Trisets are almost always done for a single body part, primarily for such complex muscle groups as the pectorals, back, or deltoids. Following are sample trisets for each of these muscle groups:

Pectorals = Incline Flyes (upper pectoral) + Cross-Bench Pullovers (general pectoral) + Cable Crossovers (inner and lower pectorals)
Back = Seated Pulley Rowing (lats) + Barbell Shrugs (traps) + Good Mornings (lower back)

competitive techniques

Deltoids = Side Laterals (medial deltoid head) + Military Press (anterior deltoid head) + Seated Bent Laterals (posterior deltoid head)

There are also giant sets, or groupings of 4-6 exercises, but I don't do giant sets in my training. They are simply too exhausting to allow me to correctly concentrate on each exercise I do in my routines. Giant sets may work quite well for you, however, so be sure to experiment with them in your training.

Peak Contraction

When your biceps muscles contract to bend your arm, they do so through a process in which thousands of individual muscle cells shorten to contract the muscles. The more you bend your arm, the greater the number of muscle cells that must shorten. A maximum number of cells will have shortened in your biceps once your arm has been fully bent.

Logic dictates that you could strengthen the contracted biceps muscle cells to a greater degree if a heavy load is placed on them when the maximum number of cells has been shortened. Unfortunately, the very nature of most biceps exercises prohibits them from placing a load on the biceps muscles when the arm is fully bent. In Standing Barbell Curls, for example, there is little or no stress on the biceps when they are fully contracted. Indeed, at the finish position of a Barbell Curl, most of the load is on the deltoids and upper back muscles, not on the biceps.

To stimulate optimum muscle hypertrophy, bodybuilders use a technique called peak contraction in which they choose exercises that place a heavy load on the working muscles when they *are* fully contracted. Often, I will hold the contracted position of such an exercise for three or four seconds to achieve an even better peak contraction effect.

In order to use peak contraction on your biceps, take a narrow undergrip on a barbell and bend over at the waist until your torso is parallel to the floor. Hang your arms straight down from your torso, and keep your upper arms motionless throughout the movement. From this position, slowly curl the barbell upward until your arms are fully bent. Hold this peak contraction position for a few seconds to enjoy the feeling of your biceps maximally contracting under a load.

Virtually every calf and latissimus dorsi exercise allows a peak contraction at the finish point of the movement. Other good peak contraction exercises include Shrugs, Upright Rows, Dumbbell Kickbacks, Pec Deck Flyes, Leg Curls, and Leg Extensions. Regular use of these movements—occasionally holding the peak contraction position for a few seconds—will help to keep your gains in muscle mass and quality coming at an optimum rate of speed.

Continuous Tension

The momentum of a fast-moving weight in any exercise can rob you of some of the muscle-building stress that the weight should provide you along its full range of motion. To prevent this—and hence to develop greater muscle quality and mass—you should always try to do some of your exercises slowly enough so you can feel the weight over the entire intended range of motion. One of the best ways to slow down a movement is to use continuous tension, a technique in which you maintain tension in your working muscles throughout the full range of motion on every rep of a set.

To illustrate this effect on yourself, lie back on a flat bench and lift a barbell off the rack into the starting position for a Bench Press. Then tense your pecs very hard and keep them under tight tension as you slowly lower the weight down to touch your chest. As the bar descends, think of your chest muscles as huge, powerful springs being compressed by the weight. At the bottom position, allow those "springs" to push the weight back to the starting point of the movement.

The tension you feel in your pecs as you do this type of Bench Press is what I mean by continuous tension. You can use such continuous tension in virtually all exercises, and regular use of continuous tension is an excellent way to bring out every potential striation in your various muscle groups.

Iso-Tension

Through long experience, bodybuilders have learned that regularly flexing a muscle quite hard, but without the added resistance of a barbell or dumbbell, adds to muscle density and muscular detail. This type of very hard flexing is called iso-tension posing contraction.

You can practice iso-tension in two ways. One is through rigorous and regular posing practice. The other consists of "rep" flexes of each muscle group, lasting 6-8 seconds. Ten to 20 such rep flexes can be done either between sets of a workout for a muscle group (as I prefer to do it), or at any other convenient time of the day. When I was working the hardest to bring up my calves, I'd flex them at various times throughout the day, and I got good results from this practice.

While I practice my posing virtually every day year-round, I generally use iso-tension regularly for only the final five or six weeks of my peaking phase. This period of time is quite adequate for gaining maximum benefit from iso-tension posing contraction.

DOUBLE-SPLIT ROUTINES

Close to a competition, you will be doing so many total sets that it becomes difficult to train the day's body parts in only one workout. You simply don't have enough energy at your command to do justice to each group in a long training session. Then, most high-level bodybuilders train twice per day for a short period of time. Such twice-daily training involves what is called a double-split routine.

The most basic form of double-split routine involves doing your workout for appropriate major muscle groups early in the day, followed by abdominals, calves, and/or forearm training in the evening. I'd recommend that the first time you experiment with a double-split routine you do it this way.

A slightly more intense form of double-split involves training twice a day two or three days per week, and only once each day the rest of the week. Assuming that you work each major muscle group three times per week prior to a competition, here is an example of such a double-split:

M-W-F (AM)	M-W-F (PM)	Tu-Th-Sa (AM or PM)
Chest	Thighs	Upper Arms
Back	Deltoids	Forearms
Calves	Abdominals	Calves-Abs

I personally use a double-split routine daily prior to a contest, training each major muscle group twice per week. For a full outline of how I train during my precontest cycle, please refer to Chapter 11.

competitive techniques

AEROBICS

Aerobic workouts prior to a competition have become quite popular with champion bodybuilders in recent years. They add greatly to the number of calories you can burn off prior to a competition, and such training sessions should be done daily prior to a contest and at least three times per week in the off-season. Aerobic workouts should last 30-60 minutes for optimum calorie-burning benefit.

My favorite form of aerobic exercise is running, and I usually run twice a day prior to a competition. I also enjoy taking an aerobic exercise class to music from time to time. Other popular forms of aerobic exercise include bicycling, stationary bicycling, and swimming. For best results, I suggest that you rotate from one form of aerobic exercise to another each workout day.

BODYBUILDING PHARMACOLOGY

It's depressing to me to realize that many bodybuilders—women included—feel that they can take a shortcut to the top simply through heavy use of "bodybuilding drugs." I have been accused numerous times of taking steroids, no doubt because, through a coupling of genetic advantages and plain hard work, I have developed a very muscular physique. But I have never taken a drug to further my bodybuilding, and I never will.

A day after I won the Ms. America title, a sample of my blood was drawn at my request and tested in a gas-liquid chromograph for the use of steroids. Gas-liquid chromotography is an extremely sensitive test which can not only detect steroid usage as far back as six or seven months, but also reveals which steroid was used. *I tested negative for the use of all steroids,* as well as for androgenic drugs, thyroid stimulants, amphetamines and other stimulants, appetite depressants, diuretics, pain killers, and every other drug that a bodybuilder might use to enhance her development.

The message I wish to get across to you is that there is no place for drug usage in bodybuilding. I've made it without using drugs,

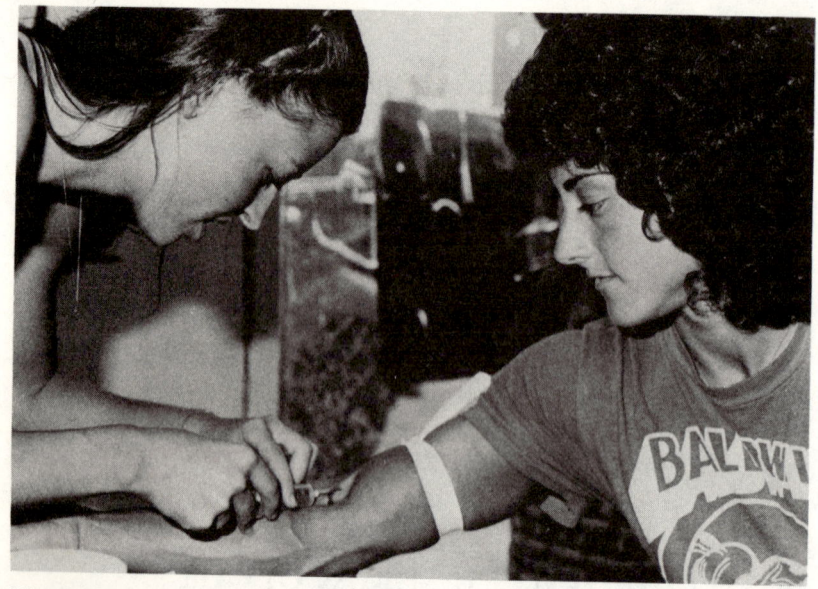

"I've frequently been accused of taking anabolic steroids, but have never touched such drugs and never will. The day after I won the America, blood was drawn for a steroid test, which proved to be totally negative." (Bill Dobbins)

and so have many other women. And the ones who take such dangerous drugs not only risk their health, but usually end up looking bloated and out-of-shape.

I am very happy that the AFWB and IFBB women's administrators are instituting drug tests as an integral part of all national and international sports. Bodybuilding is intended to build the body and improve health, and drug usage pollutes this ideal. Avoid the use of drugs at all cost!

chapter eleven
the complete cycle

In competitive bodybuilding you must mount a three-pronged attack on your muscles to achieve peak condition. These three prongs are training, diet, and psychological preparation. Certainly no male or female bodybuilder ever won a title without training. Equally as certain, diet is an important factor in the creation of a championship physique. And without a proper mental approach, all of the dieting and training in the world will not make you a winner. Therefore, in this chapter I will explain how I personally mount this three-pronged approach to successful bodybuilding.

TRAINING

Like most champion bodybuilders I train cyclically. My off-season preparation cycle begins with a 1–2-week layoff from training after a competition. By the time I've peaked for a show, I'm so saturated with bodybuilding that I can't face going into the gym. But during the layoff I'm still physically active. I run, water ski, play rugby, and get in a few games of various racquet sports. After my vacation from bodybuilding, however, it's back into the gym for six days per week of training, even during the off-season.

Early in my off-season cycle I train only once a day and schedule two training sessions per week for each body part. From my own observations, most women bodybuilders don't train hard enough. They're basically on an easy maintenance program for most of the year, then they begin to train hard only a few weeks before a show.

In the off-season, I average about 15 total sets per muscle group, compared to approximately 25 sets during my precontest cycle. I rest 45–60 seconds between sets, versus 20–30 seconds before a show. And I tend to use more basic exercises in the off-season, and more isolation movements—particularly ones with cables—during my precontest cycle.

I always use maximum poundages on at least one basic exercise per muscle group (making certain to maintain strict form), even prior to competition. In the off-season I use maximum weights in strict form on almost all of my training movements. As an example, when I am doing the Bench Press I start with 135 pounds and do eight reps as a warmup. Then I jump to 155 and do eight more reps. Finally, I increase my training poundage to 190–200 pounds (the actual weight depends on my energy level) and force myself to do 3–5 good reps.

Before a contest, I use these same poundages, because it takes heavy weights to build—or in this case to maintain—great muscle mass. Many women worry about developing large muscles if they are on a program of light weight training. Believe me, these women needn't worry. To increase my muscle mass I have to *really* push myself each training session and go for a maximum effort in at least one basic exercise per body part.

Like all bodybuilders I have weak muscle groups. In particular, my calves are less developed than other parts of my body. For more than 10 years, beginning at age 10, I was a competitive

the complete cycle

water skier. This built up my thighs and gave me great upper body development. Unfortunately, waterskiing doesn't involve using the calves because the feet are flat on the skis at all times.

In college I played rugby, which involves a great deal of sprinting, and my calves started to develop. When I began bodybuilding, they grew even more quickly, but my calves are still not up to the standard I have set for them.

Even Arnold Schwarzenegger, the best male bodybuilder of all time, had small calves at one time. But, by using muscle priority training he was able to build his calves up to the point where they were one of the best developed parts of his physique. I also use muscle priority training and it has become one of the most important aspects of my bodybuilding philosophy, especially in the off-season. Now, as soon as I get into the gym, I jump right into my calf workout. In priority training, you must train your weak body parts first, when you have the energy to hit them hardest.

Another muscle priority principle I follow is similar to one Arnold used when his calves were underdeveloped. He cut off all his training pants at the knees so he'd constantly see his calves and be reminded of how weak they were. In my case, I've taken my posing mirror off the wall and set it on the floor. When I pose, I see only my legs. This focuses my mind totally on my calves and has helped me tremendously in building them up.

During my off-season cycles, I also use the reverse of muscle priority training. For example, my back tends to develop more quickly than other body parts, so during the off-season I do just a few exercises to maintain back development. This allows me to save a lot of energy for working my weaker muscle groups. I only do my full back workout during the last 6–8 weeks before competing, but that small amount of intense training gets my back into competitive shape quite easily.

I start my precontest cycle about three months before a competition. I begin by gradually tightening my diet and progressively intensifying my training. I work each major muscle group three times per week, and I gradually do more total sets for each body part. I also do an increased amount of aerobic activity. At peak training intensity, I run two miles every morning and two or more miles every evening. And I also take several one-hour aerobic dance exercise classes each week.

I quality train, which means gradually shortening the rest intervals between sets. Combined with a strict diet and aerobic workouts, quality training gives me maximum muscle mass with sharp cuts. Obviously, my training poundages suffer a little when I am dieting and quality training, but I try to keep them as high as I can handle in good form. I never allow my training weights to drop by more than 20 pounds below my off-season poundages. If I do, I feel like I'm giving up and not trying hard enough. It hurts to train this intensely, but as the old saying goes, "No pain, no gain."

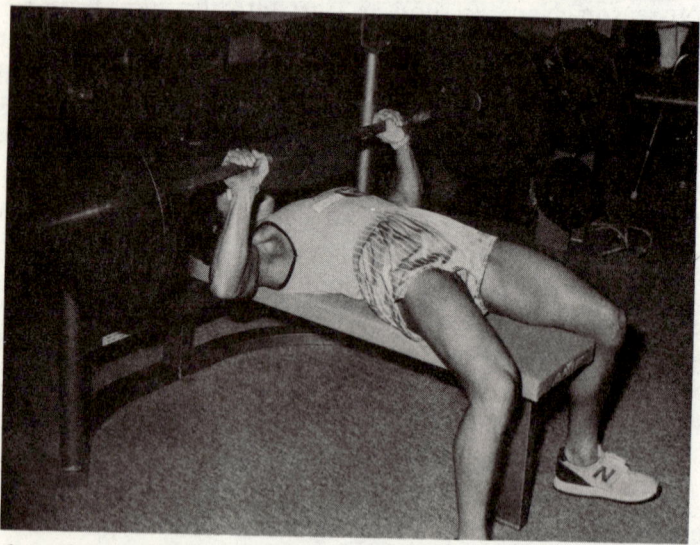

A lot of bodybuilders increase their reps in the precontest cycle, but I keep my repetitions at an average of 8–10 per set. However, I do increase my use of continuous tension and peak contraction. There's no point in letting momentum remove stress from a working muscle, so for each exercise I move the weights slowly and with full tension in my muscles over a complete range of motion.

the complete cycle

Overall, I think that using peak contraction gives me more muscle growth and hardness than does continuous tension. For example, I achieve peak contraction when I do my Leg Extensions by pausing for a slow count of two or three at the top of every repetition and completely tensing my quads. This brings out the ultimate degree of thigh muscle separation, particularly in the vastus medialis muscles which mainly come into action during the last 10-15 degrees of a Leg Extension movement.

My final muscularity training secret is my use of iso-tension contraction. Doing hard repetition flexes of each muscle group brings out striations in my muscles that otherwise would never be there. I've been using iso-tension contractions on my calves in recent months, and the results have been gratifying. I flex my calves at all hours of the day and in such unlikely places as at the dinner table, on airplanes, and in movie theaters.

Later in this chapter I will give you my exact precontest training programs for each body part. I begin my precontest cycle by doing the fewest number of sets listed for each exercise. Then I gradually add to the total number of sets for each body part, and by the final three or four weeks before the contest I'm doing five sets or so of every exercise.

Because my energy levels are so low, I usually do three or four bodybuilding workouts per day (plus two or three aerobic sessions) and work only one body part per session. I rest two or three hours between all workouts, which means I'm training, posing, or sunning virtually all day. Fortunately I have a sponsor and income from seminars and posing exhibitions, so I am able to follow this regimen for 4-6 weeks before competition.

Sometimes I will work two small body parts in one session during my precontest cycle, but usually I train only one muscle group. Then I rest and work another body part. I have to train this way, because I'm always so chronically fatigued and low on energy the last few weeks before a show that I couldn't do justice to each muscle group on even a double-split routine. Doing one body part per workout is really the only way I can train with the quality and intensity I want during my precontest cycle.

DIET

Like my training, my diet is cyclical. During the off-season I sometimes indulge myself with high-calorie foods, and my training is flexible. Then, as a contest approaches, I pay much more careful attention to my nutrition and training. Since I find it very difficult to keep my diet at precontest level, I diet intensely only two or three times a year, just before major competitions. I also diet in preparation for exhibitions, but not quite as strictly as before a contest.

While my off-season diet is relaxed, it is still nutritionally well-balanced. This is the time when I am actually building most of my muscle mass, and no bodybuilder will ever develop quality muscle tissue on an unhealthy diet. To develop muscle you must eat plenty of high-quality protein, adequate fats, enough carbohydrates to maintain training energy, and sufficient levels of vitamins, minerals, and trace elements.

I am prone to putting on body fat, so I consume only about 2,000 calories per day during the off-season. Actually, I follow my instinct in my diet as much as I do in my training. Instead of keeping close track of my diet in the off-season, I alter my food consumption according to what I sense my body needs.

Generally speaking, my off-season diet is higher in fat content, and hence higher in calories, than my diet during a precontest cycle. (Remember that one gram of fat equals nine calories, while one gram of protein or carbohydrate equals only four calories.) I indulge myself with a little junk food occasionally during the off-season, but I'm careful not to overdo it.

My off-season weakness is beer, which I really miss when I'm on my precontest diet. Obviously, I never drink it to excess, but nothing quenches my thirst like an ice-cold brew. I think that this minor, off-season pleasure is a kickback to my rugby playing days. Rugby players tend to drink gallons of beer before, during, and *after* a game!

During the off-season I try to consume about one gram of protein—or a little less—per pound of body weight. My main protein sources are chicken and other poultry, fish, eggs, a little

the complete cycle

beef, and a small amount of milk products. I avoid eating beef, cheese, eggs, or cottage cheese during my precontest diet phase because of their fat content. But in the off-season, my body needs these fats, both for general health and energy requirements.

While I am sure that a vegetarian diet is sufficient for many men and women—including bodybuilders—I build more muscle mass when I eat animal protein. However, during the off-season I get some protein from my limited intake of nuts, seeds, grains, seed sprouts, corn, potatoes, and legumes. Such vegetable-source proteins can be good if they're consumed in conjunction with animal proteins. The animal protein completes the amino acid balance of vegetable proteins and makes the vegetable proteins more assimilable by the body.

Fresh fruits and vegetables are my favorite sources of carbohydrates year-round. Fructose, the sugar found in fruits, passes very quickly into the bloodstream. So, fruit is a good source of quick energy for workouts. If you feel yourself dragging, you can even eat a piece of fruit midworkout during the off-season. Generally speaking, both fruits and vegetables are low in calories.

My other sources of off-season carbohydrate include nuts, seeds, grains (especially rice), and potatoes. In the off-season I can indulge myself with a little butter or sour cream on my baked potato. Close to a contest, of course, such fats are *verboten*.

I take vitamin and mineral supplements throughout the year. Close to a competition my diet is so strict that I lack many of the vitamins and minerals I need. To compensate for this I double or triple my vitamin and mineral supplementation during the competitive season. In particular, before a contest I increase my intake of potassium, Vitamin E, and the B-complex vitamins. Otherwise, I find that one or two multi-packs of vitamins and minerals per day are sufficient diet supplementation. Regardless of what food supplements you need, be sure to take them with your meals. This allows your body to assimilate them more efficiently.

I start dieting 8–12 weeks before a competition. Precisely when I start depends totally on how much body fat I need to lose. The

Relaxing backstage during the 1980 Ms. America prejudging with men's National Physique Committee Chairman Jim Manion (right) and her training partner Richard Baldwin, Laura appears incredibly developed even with her body totally unflexed. *Bill Dobbins*

more fat I've accumulated during the off-season, the longer I'll need to diet before a contest.

Once I begin my precontest diet, I gradually eliminate more and more foods from my daily menu, and this progressively decreases the calories I consume. Of course, I *could* jump right into a strict diet regimen, but that would be a tremendous strain on both my mind and body.

It's easier and healthier to diet sensibly for a long period than to crash diet for a couple of weeks. Personal experience has taught me that crash dieting is too hard on the mind and body, and it causes you to lose considerable muscle mass.

On my precontest diet I first cut out all junk foods and beer. Then the milk products, seeds, nuts, and grains are gradually eliminated. Next, I stop eating beef, then eggs (except for egg whites occasionally; egg whites are almost pure protein). Finally, I reduce the amount of fruit, vegetables, poultry, and fish I consume.

Ultimately, my precontest diet is virtually devoid of fat, and my daily food intake is 800–1,000 calories. I eat fish, chicken breasts (with the fatty skin removed before broiling), green salads, and two or three small servings of low-calorie fruits (e.g., melons and berries) each day. I drink water, coffee, and tea, but avoid all diet drinks and artificial sweeteners, because of their sodium content. To peak totally, I must curtail my sodium intake. I even stop eating celery, which, although low in calories, has a high sodium content. Sodium causes water retention, a major nemesis of women bodybuilders.

A week before competition I eliminate fruit from my diet. The carbohydrates in fruit cause me to retain water. During this last week before a contest I lose all of my excess water and my skin becomes very tight over my muscles.

Throughout my precontest dieting and training cycle, I use a daily skinfold pinch test and visual monitoring of my appearance to determine how quickly I'm losing fat. If I'm not losing it fast enough, I can either train more or eat less. Usually, I'll simply run more and thereby increase my metabolism of fat. This is a more practical way to reduce body fat than reducing calorie intake, because when you're eating virtually nothing before a show it's difficult to reduce body fat by eating less than nothing!

As a general rule for women bodybuilders, I suggest never reducing your caloric intake to less than 800–1,000 calories per day prior to competition. Then, if you're still not leaning out fast enough, increase your level of aerobic activity. Instead of eating less, do more training.

PSYCHOLOGY

Your mind controls your body. And how you control and program your mind has everything to do with how well you peak for a competition. As I mentioned earlier, you can actually diet and train optimally and still fail to achieve peak condition simply because you were not mentally prepared for a contest.

I'm constantly amazed at how many bodybuilders lie to themselves, or view their image in a mirror and see something totally different than a panel of judges would see. To build a symmetrical and well-proportioned physique, you *must* see yourself objectively. Recognize and admit your weak points. Then work the lagging body part mercilessly during your training.

If you can't objectively analyze your body, then you should seek expert advice from contest judges, gym owners, or other qualified individuals. The worst thing a bodybuilder can do is rely on the comments of her "gym friends." Once you've won a contest or two, it's virtually impossible for you to do wrong in their eyes. Even if your lats are nonexistent, they pat you on the back and say, "You look great, Champ!" It's far better to have someone tell you the truth, even if it bruises your ego a little.

Once you have identified your weak points you should be very positive in your approach to bringing them up to par. While most bodybuilders have inherent weaknesses in terms of muscle origins, insertions, and shape, no body part need remain glaringly weak. With the correct training approach and sufficient time, weak muscle groups will strengthen and grow.

You must also be confident and positive in your mental attitude. You must believe you can attain peak contest condition. Year-round I use the visualization technique described earlier in this book. But it's just before a competition that I use this visualization method the most. Every night before falling asleep, I vividly imagine my body in peak condition. By combining proper diet, training, and visualization, I come much closer to attaining my ultimate condition.

MY PRECONTEST PROGRAM

The following is a day-by-day and hour-by-hour breakdown of how I prepare myself for a competition.

Monday–Thursday

7:00	Rise
7:30	Run (two miles)
8:15	Breakfast
9:30–10:30	Chest Workout
	1. Bench Press: 3 × 8 (115, 145, 155 lbs.)

the complete cycle

        2. Incline Barbell Press: 3 × 8 (115 lbs.)
        3. Pec Deck Flyes: 3 × 8 (100 lbs.)
        4. One-Arm Cable Crossovers: 3 × 8 (35 lbs.)
        5. Flat-Bench Flyes: 3 × 8 (30s)

11:00–12:00	Sunbathe
12:00	Lunch
12:30–2:00	Sunbathe
2:00–3:00	Nap (and cool off, since the Florida sun is quite hot)
4:00–5:30	Abdominals Workout

        1. Incline Sit-Ups: 3 × 20
        2. Hanging Leg Raises: 3 × 15
        3. Lying Leg Raises: 3 × 15
        4. Crunches: 3 × 30

Back Workout
        1. Barbell Bent Rows: 3 × 8 (115, 125, 135 lbs.)
        2. T-Bar Rows: 3 × 8 (125 lbs.)
        3. Wide-Grip Chins: 3 × 6–8 (no added weight)
        4. Wide-Grip Lat Pulldowns: 3 × 8 (120 lbs.)
        5. Close-Grip Lat Pulldowns: 3 × 8 (120 lbs.)
        6. Seated Pulley Rowing: 3 × 8 (150 lbs.)
        7. One-Arm Cable Rowing: 3 × 8 (50 lbs.)

7:15	Run (two or three miles)
8:15	Dinner
9:30	Posing Practice
10:30	Retire

Tuesday–Friday

7:00	Rise
7:30	Run (two miles)
8:15	Breakfast
9:30–10:30	Leg Workout

        1. Leg Curls: 3 × 8 (60 lbs.)

        2. Standing Leg Curls (one leg): 3 × 8 (20 lbs.)
        3. Squats: 3 × 8 (115, 165, 215 lbs.)
        4. Hack Squats: 3 × 8 (100 lbs.)
        5. Leg Press: 3 × 8 (150, 180, 200 lbs.)
        6. Leg Extensions: 3 × 8–15 (130 lbs.)
        7. Lunges: 3 × 30 (45 lbs.)

Time	Activity
11:00–12:00	Sunbathe
12:00	Lunch
12:30–2:00	Sunbathe
2:00–3:00	Nap (and cool off)
4:00–5:30	Abdominal Workout (same as Monday–Thursday) Shoulder Workout

        1. Dumbbell Press: 3 × 8 (30s, 35s, 40s)
        2. Military Press: 3 × 8 (90 lbs.)
        3. Side Laterals: 3 × 8 (30s)
        4. Front Dumbbell Raises: 3 × 8 (30s)
        5. Seated Bent Laterals: 3 × 8 (30s)
        6. Prone Incline Laterals: 3 × 8 (25s)
        7. Upright Rowing: 3 × 8 (75, 85, 95 lbs.)

Time	Activity
7:15	Run (two or three miles)
8:15	Dinner
9:30	Posing Practice
10:30	Retire

Wednesday–Saturday

7:00	Rise
7:30	Run (two miles)
8:15	Breakfast
9:30–10:15	Calf Training

        1. One-Leg Calf Raise: 3 × 30 (no weight)
        2. Standing Calf Raise: 3 × 10 (it's a lever-type machine, so it's difficult to say what weight I am

the complete cycle

using; it is, however, quite heavy)
   3. Seated Calf Raise: 3 × 10 (200 lbs. with weight right on knees)
   4. Seated Calf Raise: 3 × 10 (50 lbs. on lever-type machine)
   5. Calf Press (on leg press machine) 3 × 15 (200 lbs.)
   6. Donkey Calf Raise: 3 × 15 (one or two people on back totalling 225-250 lbs.)

Time	Activity
11:00–12:00	Sunbathe
12:00	Lunch
12:30–2:00	Sunbathe
2:00–3:00	Nap (and cool off)
4:00–5:30	Abdominal Workout (same as on Monday-Thursday) Arm Workout

1. Close-Grip Bench Presses: 3 × 8 (110, 120, 130 lbs.)
2. Lying Triceps Extensions: 3 × 8 (75 lbs.)
3. Triceps Pushdowns: 3 × 8 (75 lbs.)
4. One-Arm Dumbbell Extensions: 3 × 8 (30 lbs.)
5. Dumbbell Kickback (one arm): 3 × 8 (35 lbs.)
6. Standing Barbell Curl: 3 × 8 (60, 70, 80 lbs.)
7. Barbell Preacher Curls: 3 × 8 (55, 65, 75 lbs.)
8. Reverse Preacher Curls: 3 × 8 (55 lbs.)
9. Alternate Dumbbell Curls: 3 × 8 (30s)
10. Concentration Curls: 3 × 8 (30 lbs.)
11. Cable Curls: 3 × 10 (25 lbs.)
12. Barbell Wrist Curls: 3 × 15 (75 lbs.)
13. Dumbbell Wrist Curls (one arm): 3 × 8 (40 lbs.)
14. Standing Barbell Wrist Curls: 3 × 8 (90 lbs.)

Time	Activity
7:15	Run (two or three miles)
8:15	Dinner
9:30	Posing Practice
10:30	Retire

On Sundays I more or less rest, but close to a competition I often do my running and extra abdominal training if I am not sufficiently cut up. Additionally, the program just listed is more or less *the minimum* I do. Frequently, I will do calf training and other types of aerobic workouts at other times of the day, over and above what is listed.

CONCLUSION

In this concluding chapter I've explained all aspects of my training philosophy. But please don't take everything I write here or say in a seminar as The Gospel According To Laura. I can only comment on training, diet, and mental conditioning from my own perspective. What works well for me may or may not work as well for you. In the final analysis, you must digest the advice I give you and then use your bodybuilding instinct to decide what works best for your unique body.

Writing this book for you has been a pleasure, but it's as far as I can personally take you in the sport. You have to pump iron, diet, and prepare yourself mentally on your own. I simply can't get into your body and do it for you. But, as you will no doubt discover, you get out of bodybuilding exactly what *you* put into bodybuilding.

Good luck with your workouts. I hope I will see you in the gym some day. But until then, go for it!

index

A

Abdominal exercises, 61, 72–77, 105, 110
Abdominal muscles, 62, 103
Advanced routines, 105–10
Aerobics, 150
AFWB Judging Guide, 117
Almond oil, 133
Amenorrhea, 18–19
American Championships, 137, 141
American Federation of Women Bodybuilders (AFWB), 117
Appearance, contestants', 115, 131–33

Arm exercises, 79–91, 110
  basic, 97
  isolation, 97
At-home training, 15
Attire, posing, 131, 132–33
Avocado oil, 133

B

Back exercises, 43–49
  basic, 97
  isolation, 97
Baldwin, Richard, 10, 23
Barbell Bent Rowing, 43, 44, 49, 59

Barbell exercises, 35-36, 37, 38-39, 44, 53, 54, 55, 62, 63, 64, 71, 79-80, 81, 89-90, 144-45
Barbell Front Raises, 55
Barbell Preacher Curls, 81
Barbell Shrugs, 49
Barbell Wrist Curls, 89-90
Baxter, Kay, 10
Bench Leg Raises, 75
Bench Presses, 35-36
   Close-Grip, 85
Benches, exercise, 35-36, 37-38, 39-40, 57, 59, 72-73, 75, 76, 82, 89-91
Best-in-the-World Championships, 9
Biceps femoris muscles, 62
   exercises for, 62, 66-67
Biceps muscles, 79
   exercises for, 44, 79-80, 82-84, 144-45
Biofeedback, 25-26, 100-101
Biomechanics, 136
Birth control, 19
Bodybuilding tripod, 15
Body fat, 19, 25, 26, 101, 113, 158
Brachialis muscles, 79, 81
Breathing Squats, 39-40
Buttocks, exercises for, 64

C

Cable Crossovers, 40
Cable Curls, 82
Calf Muscles. *See* Gastrocnemius muscles
Calf Presses, 71
Calf Raises, One-Leg, 67

Carbohydrates, 28, 134
   sources of, 28, 159
Cheating, 53, 56, 80, 144
Chest exercises, 35-41
   basic, 97
   isolation, 97
Childbirth, 18, 19
Chins, 43, 46, 59
Choreography, posing, 129
Close-Grip Bench Presses, 85
Commitment, 16
Competition, 4-5, 9, 95
   observing, 114-22
   prejudging, 114
   techniques for, 113-51
Concentration Curls, 82-84
Continuous tension, 148-49, 156-57
Contraception. *See* Birth control
Corney, Ed, 9, 124
Cross-Bench Pullovers, 39-49
Crunches, 76
Curls
   Barbell Preacher, 81
   Barbell Wrist, 89-90
   Cable, 82
   Concentration, 82-84
   Leg, 66-67
   Reverse, 79
   Standing Alternate Dumbbell, 82
   Standing Barbell, 79-80
   Standing Wrist, 90-91

D

Decline Flyes, 35
Decline Presses, 35
Dehydration, 29

index

Deltoid heads
  anterior, 51, 55–56
  medial, 51, 55, 58–59
  posterior, 51, 57, 58–59
Deltoid muscles, 41, 49, 51, 59
  exercises for, 35–36, 37, 52, 55–56, 57, 58–59
Demographics, bodybuilding, 12–13
Diaphragms, 19
Diaries
  nutrition, 23–25
  training, 23–25, 99
Diet, 15, 26–32, 158–61
Diets, 94–95
  low-carbohydrate, 134–35
  low-fat, 134
  off-season, 158
  precontest, 134–35, 159–61, 162–66
  vegetarian, 159
  weight-gain, 30–32
  weight-loss, 29–30
Donkey Calf Raises, 71–72
Drugs. *See* Pharmacology
Dumbbell exercises, 39–40, 52, 55, 57, 58–59, 64, 67, 82–84, 86, 88–89, 90–91
Dumbbell Front Raises, 55–56
Dumbbell Presses, 52
Dumbbell Shrugs, 49
Dumbbell Side Laterals, 55
Dunlap, Carla, 10, 104

E

Elliott, Lisa, 10, 104, 132
Energy, 101–2, 149
Erector spinae muscles, 43, 49

Esthetics, 2–3
Estrogen, 19
External oblique muscles, 62
EZ-Curl bars, 81, 85, 86

F

Fat
  body, 19, 25, 26, 101, 113, 158
  dietary, 27, 134, 158
  polyunsaturated, 27
  reducing, 29
Fatigue, chronic, 25–26, 98, 101
Fatigue toxins, 13
Female factors, 18–19
Femininity, 139
Fiber, 28
  sources of, 28
Five-day split routines, 103
Flat-Bench/Incline Flyes, 37–39
Floor pulleys, 54
Flyes
  Decline, 35
  Flat-Bench/Incline, 37–39
  Pec Deck, 41
Forearm muscles, 79, 91
  exercises for, 80, 81, 89–90, 110
Four-day split routines, 101–3
Front Raises
  Barbell, 55
  Dumbbell, 55–56
Fundamentals, bodybuilding, 7–19

G

Gastrocnemius muscles, 62
  exercises for, 68–69, 71, 110
Genetic potential, 32–33, 82

Giant sets, 147
Goals, 17–18
  long-term, 17–18
  short-term, 17–18
Gold's Gym, 15
Gyms, 15

H

Hack machines, 63
Hack Squats, 63
Hairstyles, 131, 132
Hamstrings. See Biceps femoris muscles
Hand positions, posing, 127
Handicaps, physical, 5
Hanging Leg Raises, 73
Health, overall, 3
Heredity, 32–33, 82
Hormones, 13, 19
Hours, training, 16
Hunger, 101
Hyperextensions, 49
Hypertrophy, 14–15, 94

I

Incline Barbell Presses, 37
Incline Sit-Ups, 72–73
Income, bodybuilding, 5
Injuries, 135–36
Insomnia, 26, 98
Instinct, training, 15–16, 24, 25–26, 99–101
Intensity, training, 13, 14, 103
  increasing, 142–49
Intercostal muscles, 62
Iso-tension, 149, 157

JKL

Jewelry, 132
Joe Weider's Muscle & Fitness *Training Diary,* 24
Judging standards, 1–2, 7–12, 114–15
Lat Pulldowns, 43, 46
Lateral Raises, 59
Latissimus dorsi muscles, 43
  exercises for, 44, 45, 46, 47, 48
  lower, 46
  upper, 46
Layoffs, 98–99, 153–54
Leg Curls, 66–67
Leg exercises, 61–73
  basic, 97
  isolation, 97
Leg Extensions, 64–66
Leg Press machines, 64, 71
Leg Presses, 64
Leg Raises
  Bench, 75
  Hanging, 73
Lifestyle, 2, 16–18
Lifting belts, 53
Lighting, posing, 126, 132
Literature, bodybuilding, 99
Lower back muscles, 49
  exercises for, 44, 45, 62
Lower leg muscles, 62
Lumbar muscles, 49
Lunges, 64
Lying Barbell Triceps Extensions, 86

M

Makeup, 131, 132, 133

index

Meats, 29
Menopause, 18
Menstruation, 18-19
Mental attitude, 15, 136-42, 161-62
Mentzer, Mike, 10
Mentzer, Ray, 10
Menu, weight-gain, 30-31
Military Presses, 53
Mineral oils, 133
Minerals, 28-29, 159
Miss Olympia, 4, 19, 25
Motivation, 2-3, 23, 99
Movements
  basic, 96-97
  isolation, 96-97
Mr. America, 10, 151
Mr. Universe, 10
Ms. America, 10-11, 16
Ms. Florida, 10
Ms. Northwest Florida, 10
Ms. Tampa, 10
Muscle & Fitness magazine, 12, 24
Muscle mass, 25, 93-96, 115
  building, 95-96
Muscle priority training, 111, 155
Muscle tone, 115
Muscularity, 12, 25, 133, 145
Music, posing, 129

N

Nautilus Leg Extension Machines, 64-66
Nutrition. *See* Diet
Nutrition Almanac, 27

O

Off-season training cycles, 94-95, 101-5, 153-54
Oil, body, 131, 133
One-Arm Cable Rowing, 48
One-Arm Pulley Rows, 48
One-Arm Triceps Kickbacks, 88-89
One-Leg Calf Raises, 67
One-Leg Toe Raises, 68
Overhead Presses, 53, 59
Overload, muscles, 14-15
Overtraining, 26, 98-99
  symptoms of, 98
Ovulation, 19

P

Pain threshold, 13
Parallel Bar Dips, 35
Partners, training, 21-23, 145
Paulik, Auby, 19
Peak contraction, 147-48, 156-57
  exercises for, 148
Peaking, 113
Pec Deck Flyes, 41
Pectoral muscles, 35, 41
  exercises for, 35-41
Perspiration, 29
Pharmacology, bodybuilding, 151
Photographs, 24-25, 125, 128-29
Pillow, 104
Posedowns, 115
Posers
  guest, 122
  male, 9, 10
Poses, compulsory, 115-17, 127

Posing, 9–11, 122–31
  free, 122, 127, 129
  practicing, 125, 149
Poundages, training, 13–14
  increasing, 17–18, 94, 95–96
  maximum, 37, 154
Precontest programs, sample, 162–66
Precontest training cycles, 94, 150, 157, 162–66
Pregnancy, 18, 19
Presses
  Bench, 35–36
  Calf, 71
  Close-Grip Bench, 85
  Decline, 35
  Dumbbell, 52
  Incline Barbell, 37
  Leg, 64
  Military, 53
  Overhead, 53, 59
Progesterone, 19
Prone Incline Laterals, 58–59
Proportions, 12, 25, 115
Protein, 26–27
  sources of, 27, 158–59
Psychology, 161–62
Pulldowns, Lat, 43, 46
Pulley Pushdowns, 86–88
Pullovers, Cross-Bench, 39–40
Pulse rate, elevated, 98
Pumps, muscle, 25, 101
Pushdowns, Pulley, 86–88
Pyramid power, 95–96

Q

Quadriceps muscles, 61–62
Quality training, 145, 156

R

Rectus abdominis muscle, 62
  exercises for, 72–73
Rep flexes, 149, 157
Repetitions
  decreasing, 95–96
  forced, 144–45
Resistance, progressive, 14, 94
Rest intervals, shortening, 145
Reverse Curls, 79
Roughage. *See* Fiber
Routines, bodybuilding, 93–111
  advanced, 105–10
  designing, 110–11
  double-split, 149–50
  off-season, 101–5
  split, 101–5
Rowing
  Barbell Bent, 43, 44, 49, 59
  One-Arm Cable, 48
  One-Arm Pulley, 48
  Seated Pulley, 43, 47
  T-Bar, 45
  Upright, 49, 54, 59

S

Sartorius muscle, 61–62
Schwarzenegger, Arnold, 155
Scoring, contest, 114–15
Seated Bent Laterals, 57, 59
Seated Calf Machine Toe Raises, 71
Seated Pulley Rowing, 43, 47
Self-analysis, 161–62
Self-coaching, 2–3
Self-discipline, 2–3
Self-image, 3
Self-sacrifice, 16, 137–38

index

Seminars, training, 99, 136
Serratus muscles, exercises for, 39–40
Shoulder exercises, 51–59
  basic, 97
  isolation, 97
Shrugs
  Barbell, 49
  Dumbbell, 49
Side Laterals
  Dumbbell, 55
  Standing Dumbbell, 59
Sit-Ups, Incline, 72–73
Six-day split routine, 103–5
Skinfold pinch test, 161
Sleep, 25, 26
Sodium, 161
Soleus muscles, 62
  exercises for, 71
Soreness, muscle, 25, 98, 101
Spotters, 36, 37
Squats, 62, 110
  Breathing, 39–40
  Hack, 63
Stamina, 13
Stances, posing, 127
Standing Alternate Dumbbell Curls, 82
Standing Calf Machine Toe Raises, 68–69
Standing Dumbbell Side Laterals, 59
Standing One-Arm Dumbbell Triceps Extensions, 86
Standing Wrist Curls, 90–91
Steroids, 151
Strength, 93–96
Suits, posing, 131, 132–33
Sunburn, 133
Supersets, 146–47
Supinator muscles, 81
Supplements, food, 28–29, 30, 159
Symmetry, 12, 115

T

Tans, 131, 133
  artificial, 133
T-Bar Rowing, 45
T-Bars, 45
Techniques
  competitive, 113–51
  intermediate, 21–33
  training intensification, 142–49
Tension, continuous, 148–49, 156–57
Testosterone, 13
Thigh muscles, 61–62
  exercises for, 62, 64, 64–66
Toe Raises
  One-Leg, 68
  Seated Calf Machine, 71
  Standing Calf Machine, 68–69
Torso exercises, 110
Training, 153–57
  at-home, 15
  intensity of, 13, 14, 103, 142–49
  off-season, 94–95, 101–5, 153–54
  quality, 145, 156
Training options, 15–16
Training to failure, 142–43
Transitions, posing, 129
Trapezius muscles, 43, 49, 51, 59
  exercises for, 44
Triceps muscles, 79
  exercises for, 35–36, 37, 85, 86–89

Trisets, 146–47

U

Universal Gym machines, 49
Upper back muscles, 57
    exercises for, 62
Upright Rowing, 49, 54, 59
US Food and Drug
    Administration, 27

V

Videotapes, 131

Visualization, 99, 139–42, 162
Vitamins, 28–29, 159
    fat-soluble, 27
    water-soluble, 29

W

Warm-ups, 110
Water, 29
Water retention, 19
Wide-Grip Chins, 46
Wilbourn, Claudia, 10
Workouts. *See* Routines